CONGRESSIONAL REDISTRICTING

New Topics in Politics

David Butler and Bruce Cain   *Congressional
Redistricting: Comparative and
Theoretical Perspectives*

Morris Fiorina   *Divided Government*

Donald F. Kettl   *Deficit Politics: Public Budgeting in
Its Institutional and Historical Context*

CONGRESSIONAL REDISTRICTING

COMPARATIVE AND THEORETICAL PERSPECTIVES

DAVID BUTLER
Nuffield College, Oxford

BRUCE CAIN
University of California, Berkeley

MACMILLAN PUBLISHING COMPANY
New York

MAXWELL MACMILLAN CANADA
Toronto

Editor: *Bruce Nichols*
Production Supervisor: *John Sollami*
Production Manager: *Pamela Kennedy*
Cover Designer: *Sheree Goodman*
Illustrations: *Publication Services, Inc.*

This book was set in 10/12 Janson by Publication Services, Inc. and was printed and bound by R.R. Donnelley & Sons. The cover was printed by NEBC.

Macmillan Publishing Company
866 Third Avenue, New York, New York 10022

Macmillan Publishing Company is part of
the Maxwell Communication Group of Companies.

Maxwell Macmillan Canada, Inc.
1200 Eglinton Avenue East
Suite 200
Don Mills, Ontario M3C 3N1

LIBRARY OF CONGRESS CATALOGING-IN-PUBLICATION DATA

Butler, David, 1924–
    Congressional redistricting: comparative and theoretical
perspectives / David Butler, Bruce E. Cain
        p.   cm. — (new topics in politics)
    Includes bibliographical references and index.
    ISBN 0-02-317585-0 (pbk.)
    1. United States. Congress. House—Election districts.
2. Election districts—United States.   3. Election districts.
I. Cain, Bruce E.   II. Title.   III. Series.
JK1341.B88   1992
328.73'07345—dc20   91-23487
                                        CIP

Printing: 1 2 3 4 5 6 7   Year: 2 3 4 5 6 7 8

Acknowledgments

We are indebted to many friends and institutions for help in this venture. We should especially mention the California Institute of Technology where we met and started an argument that culminated in these pages, as well as Nuffield College, Oxford and the Institute of Governmental Studies at Berkeley, which supported us in many ways while the book was being written; Vernon Bogdanor, Nelson Polsby, Austin Ranney, Byron Shafer, and Donald Stokes, who gave critical readings to the manuscript, Rhodes Cook of CQ and the Census Bureau, who supplied us with much material; Eunice Baek and Audrey Skeats, who helped us with research and typing, and, above all, our wives, who tolerated our psephological obsession.

D.B.
B.C.

Contents

Changing Boundaries: Myths and Realities

At the beginning of every decade, the political map of the U.S. Congress is redrawn, forcing candidates for the House of Representatives to run in districts with new boundaries, laid down after many hours of laborious negotiation and often acrimonious dispute in the state legislatures and the courts. What procedures do the line-drawers follow? What are the political consequences of their actions? Are they fair? Is there a better way of handling this complex and sensitive process?

In the pages that follow, we seek answers to these questions. The factors that must be taken into account in a "fair" redistricting are remarkably complex. There are both necessary and fortuitous conflicts between the various goals that most people think should be paramount in redistricting. We shall attempt to explain these goals in their theoretical, historical, and comparative contexts and to make suggestions for the least bad solutions to intractable dilemmas.

The prospect of new district boundaries at the beginning of every decade excites great political passions. States that expect to gain or lose seats feel their status commensurately enhanced or diminished. Political party activists regard redistricting as a critical opportunity for facilitating the election of more candidates from their party. Incumbents are quite naturally concerned for the safety of their own seats. Rapidly growing racial and ethnic groups see the new census as a chance to increase their political leverage. Lawyers and political scientists find well-compensated opportunities to exercise their skills in advocacy and analysis. Perched atop the fray,

1

public interest groups do what they can to lobby for what they believe is fair play.

In a few politically competitive states, the redistricting battles temporarily relegate all other political problems to the legislative back burner. It is natural for elected officials and large voting groups to want to defend themselves against any disadvantages brought about by changes in the electoral framework. It is right for reform groups to be concerned about the fairness of this one central aspect of the machinery of representation. And it is certainly understandable that the subject has attracted so much attention—although sometimes that excitement is out of proportion to what really is at stake.

Anxieties about the impending changes of district boundaries imbue the state elections preceding a redistricting with special importance. If the state legislature and the governorship are both in the same hands, the dominant party can pass the most favorable plan that the courts will accept. But if one party does not control all parts of the redistricting process—for example, if there is the possibility of a gubernatorial veto and the legislature lacks the votes to override it—the dominant party will have to compromise with the other party.

Total control of the redistricting process is therefore very valuable. Short of that "ideal" partisan situation, it is critical for a party to control at least one part of the process in order to force some sort of reasonable compromise upon the other party. In states where one party controls the legislature, this means winning the governorship or a majority in at least one of the houses of the state legislature. Thus, Republicans in the 1990 elections put extra resources into the gubernatorial races in Florida, Texas, and California, hoping to block the Democrat-controlled legislatures from enacting partisan redistrictings. Acknowledging the significance of redistricting, one Democratic National Committee spokesman said openly that his party cared more about these governorships in 1990 than about critical U.S. Senate races. Republicans saw things the same way. In 1989, Lee Atwater, the chairman of the Republican National Committee, observed, "If we allow ourselves to be ruthlessly gerrymandered in reapportionment as we did last time, we can forget any chance of getting control of the U.S. House of Representatives until well into the next millennium."

The fact that redistricting is linked to the decennial census leads local city officials and community activists to be vigilantly critical of the Census Bureau's findings and the assumptions that are made to allow for inevitable mistakes in counting (see pp. 54–55). If cities are inadequately enumerated, it can cost them representation in the state legislature and in Congress, as well as reducing their share of those federal grants that are apportioned by formulas based upon census figures.

Ethnic groups, especially those which include large noncitizen, indigent, and homeless populations, also closely scrutinize the census process before each redistricting. Since nonwhite immigrants are more likely to live in overcrowded, dangerous, and hard-to-locate places and tend to be especially suspicious of government officials, it is likely that normal census procedures, unaided by a special postenumeration survey, will underestimate the group's true population, thereby depriving them of their rightful share of representation. Indeed, a sophisticated statistical education is offered to those with the patience to listen to experts argue over the relative fairness of alternative methods for correcting Census Bureau figures.

In states or areas where many changes must be made at all levels of government — congressional, state legislative, and local — redistricting can become an ultrasensitive matter. If Democrats and Republicans are feuding about boundary lines for congressional districts, this can poison the negotiations over state legislative districts, and vice versa. For a while, all legislative activity in these states may be affected by the need to make redistricting deals with neighboring legislators or with party leaders. Important policy matters and pending legislation can become less pressing than the pragmatic task of bringing redistricting negotiations to a successful conclusion. For these state legislatures, the unstated motto at the beginning of each decade is "Redistricting über alles."

The ways in which redistricting is decided over those critical few months at the beginning of a decade can echo on through the courts for years to come, as happened in Indiana, California, and New Jersey during the 1980s. A "bad" redistricting can leave a legacy of bitterness between legislative colleagues, bedeviling working relationships for many years thereafter. Whatever political "benefits" the partisan 1981–82 California redistrictings may have brought to Democrats (probably three to five seats), they have to be balanced against the costs incurred by the legislature becoming more bitterly partisan immediately thereafter. In addition, Republicans were so upset at the lines the Democrats drew that they subsequently sponsored several expensive redistricting referendums and reform initiatives. California Republicans also used the redistricting issue to mobilize their faithful in a successful 1986 recall campaign against three liberal state supreme court justices, reminding their supporters that the state supreme court ruled against the Republican party in every redistricting issue that came before it during the 1980s.

It is often said that redistricting is an insider's game, and that only those with a stake in the outcome, or with a serious addiction to back room politics, follow the process closely. Redistricting is simply too arcane and esoteric a subject to excite great popular interest. Nonetheless, some citizens' groups—Common Cause, the League of Women Voters, and other "good government" groups—in their revulsion at the way redistricting is conducted are provoked into an active promotion of reform. At the end of every decade, before the next round of redistricting, many suggestions for changing the process emanate from citizen groups. Some suggest that responsibility for the process should be taken away from the politicians and given to commissions. Others propose mechanical solutions that would altogether eliminate human judgments. Still others compile lists of formal criteria that could be used to channel redistricting efforts in a more constructive direction. The extent of effort along these lines is suggested by a partial list of reform propositions put forward in statewide referendums in the 1980s, as listed in Table 1.1.

Judging by the agitation and anxiety it engenders, redistricting must matter. Certainly politicians, interest groups, party activists, the media, and would-be reformers behave as if the way in which constituency boundaries are drawn can make a key difference to their political well-being. But ironically, while the obsession with redistricting remains as strong as ever, the actual stakes are objectively less than they once were, in large measure because the constitutional constraints have become much greater. At one time, huge inequalities in district populations could be used to favor certain groups over others, giving them undue weight in state and national legislatures (Baker, 1967). But as we shall discuss later, all significant disparities in numbers have been outlawed by the American courts. Gross malapportionment—the practice of giving districts with small populations to the favored group and districts with much larger populations to other groups—is a more powerful tool of political advantage than boundary adjustments between districts of equal population. Among the alternative plans that would be acceptable to a judge applying the principle of "one person, one vote," the difference in most instances between the best and the worst plans would only alter the party balance by a handful of seats. By contrast, if districts were not constrained to be equal in population, almost any outcome from total majority control to total minority control would be possible.

Although the potential political advantage to be gained from redistricting is less than it was before 1962, when the judgment in *Baker* v. *Carr* 369 U.S. 186 transformed the scene, district boundaries can nonetheless still be drawn to favor particular parties or ethnic groups. Throughout the subsequent decade Republicans in California and Democrats in Indiana continued to feel aggrieved about the way that their districts were carved in 1981; so did African-Americans in Alabama and Latinos in Texas. How much difference does redistricting actually make to electoral outcomes?

We can get a clearer answer to this question by distinguishing between national effects and specific state or district level effects. The former are generalizations about the net impact that redistricting has upon party balance, electoral competitiveness, and "fair representation" at the national level, while the latter refer to the potential ways that boundary changes affect the probabilities of specific district or state electoral outcomes. Examples of the national level effects are those that link redistricting to the systematic causes of partisan dominance, the incumbency advantage, and the underrepresentation of racial and ethnic minorities. Redistricting reform has become for some critics the panacea for all that ails American politics. At the other extreme, a few political scientists have concluded that because the evidence of systematic effects is lacking, redistricting does not matter much. Politicians simply do not like uncertainty, they maintain, and their anxiety about boundary changes indicates less about the reality of what is at stake than about the jittery psyches of elected officials. This view, however, seems equally mistaken.

Table 1.1 A Sample of Referendum and Initiative Propositions

State	Year	Primary/ General	Prop. Number	Description	Percentage in Favor
California	1990	Primary	118	Two-thirds vote of legislature and public vote	33
			119	Establish commission	36
California	1984	General	39	Commission of retired judges (Deukmejian)	45
California	1983			Sebastiani Initiative: Qualified but was removed from ballot by state supreme court	
California	1982	General	14	Commission	46
California	1982	Primary	10	Approval of congressional districts	31
			11	Approval of state senate districts	33
			12	Approval of state assembly districts (Propositions 10–12 qualified for the ballot but were later nullified by the state supreme court)	34
California	1980	Primary	6	Constitutional amendment to Articles 4, 13, 21	56
Other States					
Idaho	1986	General	4	In 1990 reapportionment, limits senate to 30–35 members and house to not more than two times senate size; sets baseline rules for county integrity in drawing district boundaries	67

6

State	Year	Election	Number	Description	%
Oregon	1986	General	2	Modification of reapportionment procedures, legislator recall, and residence provisions	68
Vermont	1986	General	7	Change assembly reapportionment from "after each second presidential election" to after each census	75
Maine	1986	General	10	Efficiency and duties of reapportionment commission	65
Montana	1984	General	C14	Congressional district must be redistricted within 90 days of issuance of official census figures	66
Washington	1983	General	CA SJR13	Create commission for legislative and congressional redistricting	61
Oklahoma	1982	General	556	Approval of congressional districts	49
Montana	1982	General	5	Member selection for congressional redistricting commission	44
Montana	1982	General	12	State senate reapportionment commission	57
South Dakota	1982	General	Amendment A	Establishing single-member senate districts	52
Wisconsin	1982	General	2	Correcting redistricting provisions	73

SOURCES: *Initiative and Referendum Report*, June 1981–November 1987; *Initiative and Referendum Report: The Power of the People*, Fall 1986–Summer/Fall 1989; and *California Ballot Propositions, 1944–Present*, Barbara Friedrich, 1989.

7

Consider first the exaggerated claims made about the importance of redistricting. One widely held in certain Republican circles is that redistricting bias accounts for the split party control of national government (i.e., the fact that the Democrats retain control of Congress even though the Republicans have held the presidency for all but four years since 1968). The argument goes as follows: Because the Democrats control more state legislatures than the Republicans do and because most congressional redistrictings are done by state legislatures, congressional lines are systematically biased against Republican candidates. The corollary to this proposition is that if the Republicans could gain control of more state legislatures or if the redistricting process were made more neutral, Republicans would gain control of the House of Representatives.

In fact, virtually all the political science evidence to date indicates that the electoral system has little or no systematic partisan bias and that the net gains nationally from redistricting for one party over the other are very small. The most common measure of electoral bias used by political scientists is the share of seats a party would receive if it were to get 50 percent of the vote. By this standard, Gary Jacobson estimates that the Democrats would have secured 52.1 percent of the seats with 50 percent of the vote between 1946 and 1964, and 53.9 percent between 1966 and 1988. However, when he corrects for the inflated percentages resulting from uncontested seats, he finds that Democrats would have been predicted to get 42.8 percent of the seats with 50 percent of the vote before 1966 and 50.6 percent after 1966 (Jacobson, 1990). In other words, the U.S. has gone from a situation of Republican bias to one that is very close to perfectly neutral.

Other studies confirm this conclusion. King and Gelman estimate that, taking the impact of incumbency into account, the underlying bias of the electoral system is actually pro-Republican, not pro-Democratic (Gelman and King, 1990). Campagna and Grofman also find evidence of only a small degree of pro-Democratic partisan bias after the 1981 congressional redistrictings (Campagna and Grofman, 1988); they further maintain that this small bias in the swing ratio was actually less in 1982, after the redistrictings, than it was in 1980, the election before redistricting. They conclude: "Thus, for those two election years, there is no evidence to support the often-made claim that the preponderance of Democratic control of the redistricting process has significantly harmed Republican chances of controlling Congress" (p. 10). What does this small degree of bias mean? One sophisticated estimate following the 1982 election was that only 4 of the 26 seats lost by the Republicans could be directly attributed to redistricting (Robertson, 1983). In retrospect, these findings should not come as a great surprise. As we shall discuss in greater detail later in this book, in order for one party to control the redistricting process a variety of conditions must exist. The same party must not only control both houses of the legislature—which means having a majority of both houses when majority rule is employed, and more than that when there is supermajority rule—but also, if a veto is to be avoided, the governor's office as well. However, even when the institutional and political opportunities for one party to draw lines to partisan advantage are present, the incentive to gerrymander may not be very strong. The incentive to use district boundary change to partisan advantage is strongest when the state's Democrats and Republicans are in close electoral competition with one another but only one party has full control of the state's redistricting process (Cain and Campagna, 1987).

This situation is relatively rare, however, and thus partisan redistrictings—even when it is broadly defined as "whether the parties disagree over the new lines" are far less common than bipartisan ones. In 1982, only 11 of the 50 states had any serious partisan disagreement over the new congressional districts. And since some of these states were controlled by the Democrats and others by the Republicans, the net effect was smaller still. As many people have commented, the gains that gerrymandering brought to the Democrats in California in 1982 must be balanced against the losses to Democrats in states like Indiana and Arizona.

Finally, we should note that partisan gerrymandering is, to say the least, an inexact science. In an era in which party loyalty has been steadily declining, it is hard to predict whether a change in district composition will necessarily lead to a change in partisan composition. The experience of the New York state legislature in the 1970s is widely cited as a reminder that partisan redistrictings can backfire: A plan intended to give control of the New York state legislature to the Republican party was swamped by the post-Watergate backlash of 1974, and as a result the Democrats gained control of both houses (Scarrow, 1981). At the congressional level, an Indiana Republican partisan gerrymander managed to turn a 6–5 Democratic advantage into a 7–3 Democratic margin. In addition to opportunity and incentive, competence and skill seem to vary as well.

However, to say that the net national effects on partisan balance will be small in an era in which two-thirds of state governments are under split control does not mean that redistricting is without specific district- or even state-level partisan effects. In a given district under the right circumstances, redistricting can be an effective tool for partisan advantage. In the 1982 California redistricting, the so-called "Burton plan" (named after the California Democratic congressman who designed the congressional districts) altered the partisan composition of several marginal districts in critical ways, tipping the underlying party advantage toward the Democrats; in several instances, Republican incumbents were placed in the same district in order to open up seats where Democrats might make gains. Some of these changes may have only slightly facilitated gains that the Democrats would have won anyway (e.g., the Bosco and Bates districts), but others clearly created opportunities for Democratic candidates that would not have been there otherwise [e.g., the Lehman, Martinez, and Levine districts (Cain, 1985)].

In short, the decentralization of the American redistricting process serves in a curious way to check the aggregate amount of partisan bias that a predominantly legislative redistricting system can produce nationally. Most states lack the conditions for a partisan gerrymander. The cumulative effect of those few states with partisan outcomes tends to yield very little net gain for one party or the other. But in specific districts and states, partisan control can affect the line-drawing in important ways. Whether a given district is made more or less marginal, how incumbents are combined or how much territory is added to or taken away from a district can all be crucially influenced by the partisanship of the redistricting process.

A second and sometimes related claim is that redistricting is responsible for the incumbence advantage. Since most redistrictings are bipartisan, new boundary lines are usually drawn to preserve incumbent congressmen of both parties. Incumbents in these instances forego the opportunity to maximize representation for their respective parties and opt instead for seats that are safely Democratic or

Republican. Although members of Congress do not actually have a vote on their own redistricting bill (unlike state legislators), they usually cultivate sufficiently good relations with state legislators in their own party to ensure that they have input into the process. Some would argue that incumbents are reelected at rates in excess of 90 percent simply because they run within boundaries that guarantee high partisan support or, at the least, within which the incumbent is highly visible and popular.

Once again popular perception conflicts with scholarly evidence. When the rise in incumbents' advantage was first noted, there was speculation in political science literature that redistricting might account for the drop in the number of competitive seats (Tufte, 1972). However, Ferejohn found that the rate of incumbent reelection grew as much in districts which had not changed their boundaries as in those that had (Ferejohn, 1977). Grofman and Campagna, contrary to their expectations, found that the responsiveness of congressional seats (i.e., how sensitive changes in seat shares are to changes in vote shares) actually increased in the election after a redistricting, regardless of whether the lines were drawn by the legislature, the courts, or a commission. If redistricting significantly contributed to the incumbency advantage, the opposite would be true: District lines would become less responsive to small changes in vote shares after a bipartisan or incumbent's gerrymander. King's (1988) study of state legislative redistricting came to virtually the same conclusion.

These findings are surprising in the sense that if incumbents control the process of drawing boundary lines, one would expect them to use it to enhance their electoral safety. The point of a strong incumbency advantage is to secure insulation from the vicissitudes of national swing and to ensure that a small national or statewide movement in votes does not result in many incumbent defeats. Instead, these academic studies reveal the opposite. Why?

One reason may be that incumbents are really seeking to get the best deal that they can given the realities of the population changes they face. In other words, an incumbent's name recognition and the magnitude of his or her personal vote are likely to be higher in the areas they have represented for some time than in the new areas added to their seats to make them equally populated. They may exert their influence during the redistricting process to minimize the harm that comes to them from these changes, but it is possible that no change at all is generally preferable to any alteration that adds lots of new voters. This is no doubt part of the reason that states did not reapportion districts as frequently as they should have in the period before the "one person, one vote" principle was established by the courts.

There are in fact many more plausible explanations of the incumbency advantage than redistricting. The vast literature on the "personal vote" points to a number of other factors which seem to contribute more to incumbents' success: a substantial edge in campaign finance (especially from PACs and special interests), higher name recognition and visibility, and the possession of permanent staff to sustain constituency work and publicity (Fenno, 1978; Fiorina, 1977; Jacobson, 1983; Cover and Brumberg, 1982; Frantzich, 1982). Even if redistricting could be arranged to neutralize incumbency advantage by completely altering the political cartography of a state, the effect would not be permanent. We know from the literature on congressional elections that freshman congressmen work very hard during their first term in office to build up name recognition and positive images in their districts and that the second election is usually characterized by a "sophomore surge" in which the incumbent increases his or her margin of victory over the first election (Jacobson, 1990, p. 29; Cover and Mayhew, 1981).

While the aggregate relationship between the incumbency advantage and redistricting is nonexistent, that does not mean that the process does not favor specific incumbents in various ways. For instance, it is possible that system responsiveness would be even higher if incumbents had no vested interests and no input into the way district lines are drawn: Seats may not have been safer for incumbents after redistricting, but perhaps they would have become even less safe if incumbents had had no influence.[1]

Second, there are other things that incumbents want from redistricting, some of which affect them in ways that are difficult to measure. Incumbents frequently seek to keep the homes of favorite donors or the locations of good fundraising sources in their districts.

---

[1] The experience of redistricting commissions provides very little contrast with legislative redistricting in this regard since incumbents find ways to make their preferences known to commission members (Balitzer, 1980).

Sometimes incumbents will press for the inclusion of an area in which they have no support currently, but which has the potential to provide loyal support in the future. Another common demand is that the district lines cut out the house of a potential challenger — perhaps a popular state representative or a local city mayor. These requests can be very important to incumbents and may even affect the outcome of future reelection races, but will not show up in any aggregate assessments of the impact of redistricting. Thus, we should distinguish the claim that **redistricting is the cause of the incumbency advantage** from the claim that **incumbents seek and often obtain advantages from redistricting**. There is no evidence for the former and appreciable evidence for the latter.

A third and equally prevalent claim for the systematic importance of redistricting is put forth by certain racial and ethnic minority leaders. Some of them believe that the underrepresentation of blacks, Latinos, and Asians in state and national legislatures is fundamentally related to the discriminatory fashion in which district lines cut through their communities. Therefore, it is argued, if district lines were drawn with greater racial and ethnic sensitivity, U.S. minority groups could achieve their fair share of representation. Related to this claim is a much-discussed Republican strategy; it is suggested that if Republicans assist minority groups to achieve more heavily minority-dominated districts, they will systematically undermine white Democratic incumbents and hasten the realignment of congressional seats.

Democrats in Virginia, for example, worry that if black voters are concentrated by future redistrictings into a new district in the state's Tidewater area, it will weaken the base of the white Democrats in the neighboring 2nd and 4th districts (*Congressional Quarterly*, Jan. 27, 1990). To many white Democrats, it is self-serving of the Republicans to offer map-drawing assistance to minority groups and shortsighted of progressive minority groups to play into Republican hands by concentrating Democratic party support into fewer districts.

The process of creating seats with even heavier minority domination (known in the courts as "majority minority seats") has in fact been going on for close to two decades. Outside the South, there are now only a few large concentrations of Latino or black voters still split among the districts of white incumbents, and most of these are in areas of high immigration growth. Blacks in California, for instance, can realistically expect to retain only their current share of congressional seats throughout the 1990s.

In the South, however, the potential for disruption is greater, because there are still many rural black neighborhoods which could in principle be united to create majority black congressional districts. Frank Parker, director of the Voting Rights Project of the Lawyers' Committee for Civil Rights Under Law, believes that redistricting on a racial or ethnic basis might eventually lead to as many as a dozen more black and Latino congressmen. Benjamin Ginsberg, chief counsel for the Republican National Committee, has been quoted as saying that it could lead to doubling the number of black congressmen from the 25 elected in 1988 (*Congressional Quarterly*, June 2, 1990).

But even under the most optimistic scenario, any increase in a minority group's representation will still fall far short of giving them proportional representation in Congress. This is especially true of Latinos for a variety of important demographic reasons. The Latino population includes a large number of noncitizens. Even those who are legal aliens face a lengthy period before they can become naturalized citizens (Pachon, 1991). The Latino population is also younger on average than other racial and ethnic groups, with many who are ineligible to vote by reason of age. Finally, disadvantages in education and income lead to lower rates of participation, even among those who are eligible to vote.

Redistricting is important for the power of minority groups in the sense that nearly all Latino and black representatives at the state and national level are elected from minority-dominated seats. Until the arrival of Gary Franks from Connecticut in 1990, no black had been elected to the House of Representatives in a district without a substantial black population. Thus, most future gains in minority representation are likely to come from districts that intentionally or accidentally acquire a nonwhite majority. However, it is important to put these gains in a realistic perspective. The low ratio of voters to population and the fact that minority neighborhoods are sometimes too dispersed to be grouped into a single district will put severe limits on the degree to which affirmative action gerrymandering, as it is sometimes referred to, will actually remedy minority under-representation in a significant way. It is also worth remembering that, in some situations, a minority may exercise more influence by having substantial blocks of voters putting pressure in a number of "white" districts than by having a single representative of their own. In sum, the excitement over redistricting sometimes leads people to exaggerate the possibilities that a new census will bring. Parties dream of realignment through better redistricting. Reformers hope to restore competitiveness and to strike a blow against the incumbency advantage by overthrowing the traditional process of drawing lines. Some minority leaders see redistricting as the best route to full political empowerment. But while there are indeed real partisan, incumbent-related, and racial/ethnic reapportionment effects, there are equally significant constraints. Discussions of systematic redistricting tend to ignore how the federal structure and other more powerful factors in the electoral system dampen its impact. It is inaccurate to think of one overall congressional redistricting at the beginning of each decade. Rather, there are fifty congressional redistrictings and thousands of state and local redistrictings, each conducted under different conditions and constraints. As we shall see, although the Supreme Court has done much to make the process more uniform in these different settings, there is still a great deal of variation. The realities of redistricting are important, but they are less dramatic than the myths and more specific to particular political circumstances.

Conclusion

As America enters each new round of redistricting, it is time to bear in mind what is really at stake in redistricting and to sort out myths from realities, for there are few subjects which create more misunderstanding, even in sophisticated legal and political circles. Although redistricting is not the cause of all that plagues the U.S. Congress, it still matters a great deal. The process as much as its consequences has major implications for the body politic. In order to understand these, it is first necessary to place redistricting in its historical context and to set out the various procedures that have been followed as well as the technical problems involved. Then we can explore the fundamental issues and values and their necessary contradictions which make the quest for an indisputably fair and acceptable outcome so controversial. By looking at how other countries have tackled the problem, we can better appreciate the uniqueness of the American approach and ask whether the solutions that foreigners have found so useful would work within the U.S. political system and culture.

C H A P T E R 2

REDISTRICTING: 1790 TO 1990

Congressional redistricting has a long, notorious history, marked by much political controversy and seemingly endless litigation. Since the early days of the republic, it has been a lively issue, with states, localities, and—most recently—various electoral groups expressing acute anxiety about being underrepresented. There are two distinct elements to this problem: The first, **apportionment**, concerns how many seats each state should have, and the second, **redistricting**, concerns how the boundaries within each state should be drawn. Each element has its own history, evolving along separate but parallel paths.

The history of reapportionment in America can be summarized as a quest for more exact equality in representation. Along the way, the meanings of the terms "more exact" and "equality" have changed considerably: "More exact" is now equivalent to mathematical equality, and representational "equality" has been expanded to include groups as well as individuals. Apportionment controversies have centered exclusively on the "more exact" equality issue—specifically, on formulae used to allocate congressional districts to states. By comparison, the redistricting part of the process has raised both kinds of concerns, that is, how equal districts should be and what kind of equality should be protected.

Apportionment in Historical Perspective

Over the first 120 years of U.S. history, Congress, before allocating districts to states, had to decide how many districts there should

17

be. Until 1910, Congress allowed itself to grow in order to accommodate new states and a rapidly increasing population. There were repeated modifications in the rules determining size. These are summarized in Table 2.1. Initially one seat was allowed for each 33,000 of population; in 1830 the figure was changed to 47,700 and in 1840 to 70,680. This led the House to swell from 106 members in 1790 to 242 in 1830 and to 391 in 1900. In a self-denying ordinance, Congress decided in 1910 to set a permanent ceiling of 435 on its membership. As a result, by 1990 each congressman had a district with a population, on average, of 570,000.

The authority for the reallocation of seats lies in Article I, Section 2 of the Constitution. This provides that

> Representatives shall be apportioned among the several states... according to their numbers.... The actual Enumeration shall be made within three years after the first meeting of the Congress and within every subsequent term of ten years in such manner as they shall by law direct.

The Fourteenth Amendment, ratified in 1870, confirmed this provision and added that, if any male citizen's right to vote was abridged, the representation of the state could be proportionately reduced (though action was never taken on this basis).

In determining how many districts each state should have, it is not enough to say that the number should be proportional to the state's population, because the statistics leave awkward residues. In 1980, Nevada, with its 787,000 population, and Maine, with its 1,125,000, were each allotted two seats, while South Dakota, with 690,000, got only one. This produced very unequal district sizes. For instance, congressional districts in Maine had an ideal population of 563,000, Nevada 393,000, and South Dakota 690,000.

However, if state boundaries are to be respected, there is no escape from this dilemma. Ever since 1790 there have been arguments over the way seats should be apportioned to states. As Table 2.1 shows, five different methods have been followed. They have all produced broadly similar and proportionate outcomes. But states losing representation or failing to gain more have always been sensitive about the fairness of the process. The complex Huntingdon system, in force since 1950, has on the whole minimized objections,

Table 2.1   A Historical Summary of Apportionment Procedures

1790–1830
Seats were allocated to states at the rate of one to each quota of population. (The quota was 33,000 in 1790 and rose to 47,700 in 1830.) Any fractions of a quota were ignored. The House grew progressively from 106 to 242 members.

1840
Seats were allocated on a quota of 70,680, but any state with a surplus fraction of a quota over 0.50 was given an extra seat. There were 232 members.

1850–1900
The number of seats was decided in advance (it rose from 237 in 1850 to 390 in 1900) and a quota was determined by dividing the total population by this number. Seats were allocated to states on the basis of the quota. Any spare seats left over were then distributed in turn to the states with the largest fraction of a quota left over. (This was known as the Vinton system.)

1910–1940
The size of the House was permanently fixed at 435. Seats were allocated by giving each of the 48 states one seat and then awarding the remaining 387 in succession to the state with the largest remaining quota.

1950–
The 435 seats were allocated by giving each state one seat and then awarding the remaining 385 in succession, under a priority numbers formula, based on a division of each state's population by $n(n-1)$, n being the number of seats given so far to the state. (This method is named after its inventor, Edward Huntingdon of Harvard University.)

although there are those who argue that it favors the small states over the large. A reversion to the Vinton scheme, in force from 1850 to 1900, would transfer two or three seats from the small states to the bigger ones. The disputes over the best formula, which were at a peak in the 1840s, came back with a vengeance after the 1920 census. Congress's failure to agree on an apportionment bill led to the only decade in U.S. history without any congressional reapportionment. The result, however, was a permanent settlement. In 1929 an act provided that seats would be apportioned among the states automatically if Congress did not act promptly once the census figures were available.

Table 2.2 shows how seats have been allocated between the states over the past 200 years. Some remarkable variations are recorded. The oscillating fate of New York (up from 10 in 1790 to 40 in 1830, down to 21 in 1860, up to 45 in 1930, and now down to 31) contrasts with the spectacular growth of California in the past sixty years (up from 11 seats in 1930 to 52 seats in 1992). It is notable that, apart from Delaware and Wyoming with their single seats, New Hampshire is the only state to have retained the same number of congressmen for a century. Few of the large states have failed to have their representation changed every decade—and none with over 14 seats has remained the same for more than two decades. In the early days of the United States the dislocations of reapportionment were limited by the steady enlargement of the House on the basis of population increase. Until 1830, there were only four instances where any state had its representation reduced. After that, losers became much more common. Reapportionment obviously transformed the regional balance of power. The original thirteen states sank from 100 percent of representation in 1790 to 66 percent in 1830 and to 42 percent in 1870; their representation dropped to only 33 percent after the 1990 changes.

California's share of congressmen jumped from 5 percent in 1930 to 12 percent in 1992. Between 1949 and 1992 nearly sixty seats will have shifted from the frostbelt to the sunbelt. These broad geographic alterations in the legislative weight of different states and regions have had far more impact on the agenda of politics than the detailed rearrangement of constituency boundaries within states.

Table 2.2 Changes in State Allocations of Congressional Districts, 1789–1990[a]

	Constitution 1789[b]	1790	1800	1810	1820	1830	1840	1850	1860	1870	1880	1890	1900	1910	1930[c]	1940	1950	1960	1970	1980	1990
Ala.	—	—	—	1[d]	3	5	7	7	6	8	8	9	9	10	9	9	9	8	7	7	7
Alaska	—	—	—	—	—	—	—	—	—	—	—	—	—	—	—	—	1[d]	1	1	1	1
Ariz.	—	—	—	—	—	—	—	—	—	—	—	—	—	1[d]	1	2	2	3	4	5	6
Ark.	—	—	—	—	—	—	1	2	3	4	5	6	7	7	7	7	6	4	4	4	4
Calif.	—	—	—	—	—	—	—	2[d]	3	4	6	7	8	11	20	23	30	38	43	45	52
Colo.	—	—	—	—	—	—	—	—	—	1[d]	1	2	3	4	4	4	4	4	5	6	6
Conn.	5	7	7	7	6	6	4	4	4	4	4	4	5	5	6	6	6	6	6	6	6
Del.	1	1	1	2	1	1	1	1	1	1	1	1	1	1	1	1	1	1	1	1	1
Fla.	—	—	—	—	—	—	1[d]	1	1	2	2	2	3	4	5	6	8	12	15	19	23
Ga.	3	2	4	6	7	9	8	8	7	9	10	11	11	12	10	10	10	10	10	10	11
Hawaii	—	—	—	—	—	—	—	—	—	—	—	—	—	—	—	—	1[d]	2	2	2	2
Idaho	—	—	—	—	—	—	—	—	—	—	—	1[d]	1	2	2	2	2	2	2	2	2
Ill.	—	—	—	1[d]	1	3	7	9	14	19	20	22	25	27	27	26	25	24	24	22	20
Ind.	—	—	—	1[d]	3	7	10	11	11	13	13	13	13	13	12	11	11	11	11	10	10
Iowa	—	—	—	—	—	—	2[d]	2	6	9	11	11	11	11	9	8	8	7	6	6	5
Kan.	—	—	—	—	—	—	—	—	1	3	7	8	8	8	7	6	6	5	5	5	4
Ky.	2	2	6	10	12	13	10	10	9	10	11	11	11	11	9	9	8	7	6	7	6
La.	—	—	—	1[d]	3	3	4	4	5	6	6	6	7	8	8	8	8	8	8	8	7
Maine	—	—	—	—	7[d]	8	7	6	5	5	4	4	4	4	3	3	3	2	2	2	2

(cont'd)

21

Table 2.2 *(continued)*

	Constitution 1789[b]	1790	1800	1810	1820	1830	1840	1850	1860	1870	1880	1890	1900	1910	1930[c]	1940	1950	1960	1970	1980	1990
Md.	6	8	9	9	9	8	6	6	5	6	6	6	6	6	6	6	7	8	8	8	8
Mass.	8	14	17	13[e]	13	12	10	11	10	11	12	13	14	16	15	14	14	12	12	11	10
Mich.	—	—	—	—	—	1[d]	3	4	6	9	11	12	12	13	17	17	18	19	19	18	16
Minn.	—	—	—	—	—	—	—	2[d]	2	3	5	7	9	10	9	9	9	8	8	8	8
Miss.	—	—	—	1[d]	—	—	4	5	5	6	7	7	8	8	7	7	6	5	5	5	5
Mo.	—	—	—	—	1	2	5	7	9	13	14	15	16	16	13	13	11	10	10	9	9
Mont.	—	—	—	—	—	—	—	—	—	—	1[d]	1	1	2	2	2	2	2	2	2	1
Neb.	—	—	—	—	—	—	—	—	1[d]	1	3	6	6	6	5	4	4	3	3	3	3
Nev.	—	—	—	—	—	—	—	—	1[d]	1	1	1	1	1	1	1	1	1	1	2	2
N.H.	3	4	5	6	6	5	4	3	3	3	2	2	2	2	2	2	2	2	2	2	2
N.J.	4	5	6	6	6	6	5	5	5	7	7	8	10	12	14	14	14	15	15	14	13
N.M.	—	—	—	—	—	—	—	—	—	—	—	—	—	1[d]	1	2	2	2	2	3	3
N.Y.	6	10	17	27	34	40	34	33	31	33	34	34	37	43	45	45	43	41	39	34	31
N.C.	5	10	12	13	13	13	9	8	7	8	9	9	10	10	11	12	12	11	11	11	12
N.D.	—	—	—	—	—	—	—	—	—	—	1[d]	1	2	3	2	2	2	2	1	1	1
Ohio	—	—	1[d]	6	14	19	21	21	19	20	21	21	21	22	24	23	23	24	23	21	19
Okla.	—	—	—	—	—	—	—	—	—	—	—	—	5[d]	8	9	8	6	6	6	6	6

State																					
Ore.	—	—	—	—	—	—	—	—	1[d]	1	1	2	2	3	3	4	4	4	4	5	5
Pa.	8	13	18	23	26	28	24	25	24	27	28	30	32	36	34	33	30	27	25	23	21
R.I.	1	2	2	2	2	2	2	2	2	2	2	2	2	3	2	2	2	2	2	2	2
S.C.	5	6	8	9	9	9	7	6	4	5	7	7	7	7	6	6	6	6	6	6	6
S.D.	—	—	—	—	—	—	—	—	—	—	2[d]	2	2	3	2	2	2	2	2	1	1
Tenn.	—	1	3	6	9	13	11	10	8	6	10	10	10	10	9	10	9	9	8	9	9
Texas	—	—	—	—	—	—	2[d]	2	4	6	11	13	16	18	21	21	22	23	24	27	30
Utah	—	—	—	—	—	—	—	—	—	—	—	1[d]	1	2	2	2	2	2	2	3	3
Vt.	—	2	4	6	5	5	4	3	3	3	2	2	2	2	2	1	1	1	1	1	1
Va.	10	19	22	23	22	21	15	13	11	9	10	10	10	10	9	9	10	10	10	10	11
Wash.	—	—	—	—	—	—	—	—	—	—	1[d]	2	3	5	6	6	7	7	7	8	9
W.Va.	—	—	—	—	—	—	2[d]	—	—	3	4	4	5	6	6	6	6	5	4	4	3
Wis.	—	—	—	—	—	—	—	3	6	8	9	10	11	11	10	10	10	10	9	9	9
Wyo.	—	—	—	—	—	—	—	—	—	—	1[d]	1	1	1	1	1	1	1	1	1	1
Total	65	106	142	186	213	242	232	237	243	293	332	357	391	435	435	435	437[f]	435	435	435	435

[a]Years of census. Apportionment effective with congressional election two years after census. [b]Original apportionment made in Constitution, pending first census. [c]No apportionment was made in 1920. [d]These figures are not based on any census but indicate the provisional representation accorded newly admitted states by the Congress, pending the next census. [e]Twenty members were assigned to Massachusetts, but seven of these were credited to Maine when that area became a state. [f]Normally 435, but temporarily increased two seats by Congress when Alaska and Hawaii became states. SOURCE: *Biographical Directory of American Congress* and Bureau of the Census.

Early Redistricting Practices

Redistricting has always been left to state legislatures. Washington has been slow to interfere. However, in 1842 Congress did enact that representatives should be "elected by districts of contiguous territory equal in number . . . [to the state's entitlement], no district electing more than one representative." In 1872 the Reapportionment Act said that districts should contain "as nearly as possibly an equal number of inhabitants." In 1901 the words "compact territory" were added. But the House was reluctant to involve itself in the actual process of redistricting. As a House committee reported in 1901:

> Your committee is therefore of opinion that a proper construction of the Constitution does not warrant the conclusion that by that instrument Congress is clothed with power to determine the boundaries of Congressional districts, or to revise the acts of a State Legislature in fixing such boundaries; and your committee is further of opinion that even if such power is to be implied from the language of the Constitution, it would be in the last degree unwise and intolerable that it should exercise it. To do so would be to put into the hands of Congress the ability to disfranchise, in effect, a large body of the electors. It would give Congress the power to apply to all the states, in favor of one party, a general system of gerrymandering. It is true that the same method is to a large degree resorted to by the several states, but the division of political power is so general and diverse that notwithstanding the inherent vice of the system of gerrymandering, some kind of equality of distribution results.

The states have very diverse traditions of redistricting linked in some cases to their early history. Representation in colonial legislatures—as in their parent, the House of Commons—was based on communities, not on numbers. Constituencies varied greatly in size. But by the late eighteenth century, many people, Jefferson and Madison notable among them, had shown themselves very conscious of the anomalies. Although the Constitution made no reference to how the states should draw their congressional districts, "there is the evidence that those who framed and ratified the Constitution intended that the House of Representatives have as its constituency a public in which the votes of all its citizens are of equal weight" (Hacker, 1964, p. 14).

In New Hampshire, Vermont, and, to a lesser extent, in Massachusetts and Connecticut, the town meeting provided the basis for representation in the state legislature. To this day, New Hampshire has almost 400 members in its lower house (one per 2,000 population) in contrast to New York's 150 (one per 117,000) or California's 80 (one per 372,000). The compromises necessary to agreeing on each state's boundaries and constitution led to understandings about the representation of outlying areas or of particular cities, and these continued for many decades to influence the drawing of constituency boundaries. Georgia developed its unique county unit system which, until the 1960s, guaranteed an exceptional weight for rural areas in the state legislature.

In the early days, some states elected their representatives "at-large," or in multimember groupings, but the use of single-member districts became more prevalent and the idea that districts should be roughly equal in numbers also spread. The constitutions of a majority of states from the start provided for equal representation of populations, at least in the lower house, though sometimes this was qualified by guaranteed representation for particular areas, regardless of population. State upper houses were sometimes exempt from such provisions, on the analogy of the U.S. Senate.

However, states often nullified the explicit provisions of their constitution by failing to carry out regular redistricting. There was a natural temptation to inaction. Incumbents disliked having their constituencies altered, and any redistricting was bound to produce political and personal tensions. But the longer redistricting was put off, the more drastic and dislocating any change was bound to be. The boundaries for the Alabama, Tennessee, and Delaware state legislatures stayed unchanged for the first sixty years of this century and nine other states made no alterations between 1930 and 1960. [1] In the state legislatures of Vermont, Connecticut, New Hampshire, and Georgia, there were some state districts that contained 100 times the population of others.

---

[1] The five states established under the Northwest Ordinance as well as the fourteen that followed all included some kind of reference to equal representation. See *The Book of the States 1960–61*, pp. 54–58.

The drive to remedy such gross anomalies was slow in coming. At the congressional level, this was because serious anomalies were limited in number.[2] After the 1960 redistribution, carried out by state legislatures without any major court-imposed constraints, all but 40 of the 435 House seats were within 15 percent of the national average. By the standard then prevailing in Britain, Australia, and Canada, and in some U.S. state legislatures, this variance was trivial. But the exceptions could be substantial. There were two seats that contained more than twice their state quota (in Texas and in Georgia) and two that contained less than half their state quota (in Arizona and Colorado). There were 15 states which included districts with either an excess or a deficit of more than 50 percent compared to the state quota. A number of congressional districts, in short, fell significantly short of the equal population goal.

The Court and the "Equal Population" Revolution

For a long time, the Supreme Court did not seriously enter the discussion of redistricting. The first significant case was *Wood* v. *Brown* 287 U.S. 1,8 in 1932, when the Supreme Court firmly refused to invalidate a Mississippi law that had created districts of unequal population. Four justices went further and asserted that the Court did not have jurisdiction over redistricting. In 1946 Professor Colegrove, a political scientist at Northwestern University, took suit against the state of Illinois, because the 7th District in which he lived had 914,000 population as against the 112,000 in the nearby 5th District. He argued that this violated the "equal protection of the laws" laid down by the Fourteenth Amendment. By four votes to three, the U.S. Supreme Court threw out the case of *Colegrove* v. *Green* 328 U.S. 549 (1946), because the issue was, in Justice Frankfurter's words:

[2] Some of the exceptions were due to the necessary problems posed by respect for state boundaries, leaving small states far from the national average. There was also the interesting case of South Dakota with its two seats; two-thirds of the population was in the fertile east of the state, while the remaining third, separated by 200 miles of desert, lived in the west on the Black Hills. It seems to have been to the satisfaction of all concerned, congressmen and voters alike, that the two areas should each have their own representative despite the disparity in numbers.

of a peculiarly political nature and therefore not meant for judicial interpretation.... The short of it is that the Constitution has conferred upon Congress exclusive authority to secure fair representation by the states in the popular House and has left to that House determination whether states have fulfilled their responsibility. If Congress failed in exercising its powers, whereby standards of fairness are offended, the remedy lies ultimately with the people.... To sustain this action would cut very deep into the very being of Congress. Courts ought not to enter this political thicket. The remedy for unfairness in districting is to secure state legislature that will apportion properly, or to invoke the ample powers of Congress.

In 1950, in *South* v. *Peters* 339 U.S. 276 (a case involving the county unit system of voting in Georgia), the Supreme Court confirmed its opinion that such electoral matters were outside its jurisdiction.

It was therefore a great surprise when, in 1962, the whole issue of redistricting was transformed by the Supreme Court's finding in the case of *Baker* v. *Carr* 369 U.S. 186. This case, brought by ordinary Tennessee city dwellers, argued that the gross inequalities in constituency size in the state assembly (there had been no redistricting since 1901) violated both the Tennessee constitution and the Fourteenth Amendment. The Supreme Court, by six votes to two, decided that it had jurisdiction, finding for the underrepresented city dwellers. Justice Frankfurter objected, presciently, that the decision would "catapult the Courts into a mathematical quagmire." As it turns out, all redistricting in America since the *Baker* v. *Carr* decision has been conducted with an eye to what the Courts might say about the proposals.

What *Baker* v. *Carr* did was to remove the barrier placed by the Supreme Court when it ruled in *Colegrove* v. *Green* that malapportionment was a political question and therefore not justiciable. As one legal commentator has pointed out, the "political question" doctrine had been so ambiguously defined prior to *Baker* v. *Carr* that it was taken by some to mean that the Court should avoid all issues involving political matters (Lowenstein, 1989). By rejecting that broad meaning and by distinguishing **the defense of political rights** from **imprudent intervention into political disputes,** the Court cleared the way for legal challenges to state apportionment practices based on the equal protection clause of the Fourteenth

Amendment. A year later, 26 states had adopted new reapportionment plans for at least one of their chambers (*California Redistricting*, 1980, p. 84). In a flurry of cases decided in 1964, the Court invalidated thirteen state legislative plans across the country for having excessive population deviations.[3] This shift in Court doctrine was so dramatic and the political stakes were so critical that the action of Court intervention caused a vigorous reaction by the congressional opponents of "one person, one vote." In the summer of 1964, there were 130 resolutions and bills introduced before Congress aimed at restoring congressional jurisdiction over redistricting, delaying or staying state compliance with Court decisions, or proposing constitutional guidelines for redistricting (*California Redistricting*, 1980, p. 85). In the end, all of these measures failed, including a constitutional amendment by Senator Dirksen of Illinois that would, among other things, have given states the power to apportion one house of the state legislature on a nonpopulation basis. The so-called Dirksen Amendment did get a plurality of votes in the Senate but failed to achieve the required two-thirds majority.

In a relatively short period of time after the Supreme Court's decision in *Baker v. Carr*, the power to determine the broad approach to redistricting passed from Congress and the state legislatures to the courts. Redistricting history after 1962 has been primarily driven by legal decisions. During the 1970s and 1980s, in a series of separate decisions, the Supreme Court's thinking on redistricting evolved in three main directions. First, it continued to grapple with a number of loose ends concerning the meaning of "one person, one vote." Second, it inched cautiously toward closer inspection of the thorniest problem in the political thicket—partisan gerrymandering. And finally, it was forced to interpret the continually evolving Voting Rights Act as it applied to redistricting minority neighborhoods.

---

[3] Including Alabama (*Reynolds v. Simes*), New York (*WMCA, Inc. v. Lomenzo*), Maryland (*Maryland Committee v. Tawes*), Virginia (*Davis v. Mann*), Delaware (*Roman v. Sincock*), Colorado (*Lucas v. 44th Colorado General Assembly*), Washington (*Meyers v. Thigpen*), Ohio (*Nolan v. Rhodes*), Oklahoma (*Williams v. Moss*), Illinois (*Germano v. Kerner*), Michigan (*Marshall v. Hare*), Idaho (*Hearn v. Symlie*), Connecticut (*Pinney v. Batterworth*), and Iowa (*Hill v. Davis*).

Changes in the Meaning of Redistricting Equity

As the Court has struggled with the issue of representation over the last quarter of a century, the concept of the right to vote in the United States has undergone several gradual but substantial changes. The basic voting right lies in the freedom to possess and exercise the franchise. Throughout the nineteenth and twentieth centuries, the right to vote in the U.S. has been progressively extended, as it has been in Great Britain and other democracies, to classes of resident citizens who had previously been excluded from electoral participation, including non-property owners, women, and African-Americans. The Voting Rights Act in 1965 secured the right to vote for all age-eligible citizens by eliminating various obstructions to voting, such as the arbitrarily administered poll taxes and literacy tests which were widely used in the South.

However, the central issue in the post-1962 redistricting cases was not the right to the franchise *per se*. Rather, the debate focused on another aspect of the right to vote, the right to an equally weighted vote. Specifically, how equal should the populations of congressional and legislative districts be? Second, on what basis should equality be determined? And, third, over which units of government should this protection be extended?

The population disparities in the early redistricting cases were substantial. In *Baker* v. *Carr*, the Tennessee legislature had neglected to change its district boundaries since 1901, leaving the lower House districts with a 23 to 1 disparity between the largest and smallest districts and the Senate districts with a 6 to 1 disparity. In *Reynolds* v. *Sims* 377 U.S. 533 (1964), the case concerning the Alabama state legislature, the range in district populations was 16 to 1 for the House and 41 to 1 for the Senate. The disparities were somewhat less but still significant in the earliest congressional cases. The range of the Georgia districts in *Wesberry* v. *Sanders* 376 U.S. 1 (1964) was approximately 3 to 1, the population varying from 272,154 in the rural 9th District to 823,860 in the Atlanta-based 5th district. In the context of these large population variances, which almost always favored rural over urban interests, the Court reasoned that the right to vote was not equal if people voted in such unequally populated districts. Since the weight of an individual's vote varies inversely with the size of an electorate, a vote in a large district has less value than a vote in a small one. In order to have equally weighted votes, the districts must have equal populations. But having ruled in *Wesberry* v. *Sanders* and *Reynolds* v. *Sims* that districts should be equal, the next logical question was how equal must districts be in order to guarantee voters "equal protection" under the Fourteenth Amendment? Also, how much flexibility in the equal population rule should there be in order for states to pursue traditional goals such as maintaining a balance of rural and urban interests, or respecting city and county lines? The Supreme Court responded to these issues by developing two standards of population equality. Drawing upon Article I, Section 2 of the Constitution, the standard for congressional districts was made much stricter and less flexible than the one for state legislatures. In the famous words of its decision in *Wesberry* v. *Sanders*, the Court said that, "as nearly as practicable," one man's vote in a congressional election should be worth as much as another's. Population equality, in short, was to be placed coequally with contiguity above all other goals in the ordering of the congressional redistricting priorities. As a primary criterion, it could not be traded off with alternative considerations such as respect for city and county lines or compactness.

This message was reinforced in a Court decision which just preceded the 1970 census and the next round of redistrictings. In *Kirkpatrick* v. *Preisler* 394 U.S. 526 (1969), the Court ruled that states had to make a good faith effort to achieve exact mathematical equality; they had to show why any deviation from perfect equality was unavoidable or justified by good state reasons. The Court's rulings in these cases had a visible effect on the 1971 redistrictings. Whereas in 1962, only nine districts out of 435 deviated by less than 1 percent, 285 of them did in 1972 (*Congressional Quarterly* B, 708). The threat that the Court might strike down the legislature's congressional redistricting plan if one with smaller deviations was available was realized in *White* v. *Weiser* 412 U.S. 783 (1973), a case involving Texas congressional districts. The total population deviations which the federal panel of three judges found to be excessive in this case were just under 5 percent, far less than those in

Wesberry v. *Sanders* (where the deviations were 300 percent between the largest and smallest districts). In a sign of things to come, the Court opted for a plan with a total maximum deviation of 0.149 percent. In retrospect, the logic of *Kirkpatrick* v. *Preisler* gave an additional impetus to the quest for population equality. The goal of equality became important not only for its own sake, but also as a means of correcting things the courts did not like about specific redistricting plans without directly having to enunciate standards on difficult issues such as party fairness. In a similar fashion, the Court rejected a plan in *Karcher* v. *Daggett* 426 U.S. 725 (1983) with trivial population differences (0.69 percent) because it did not like the political purpose that seemed to lie behind them. In other words, a plan with "better" justifications and smaller deviations might be favored over lines with tiny but unjustified population deviations. As a consequence of these Court decisions, it is quite likely that congressional plans in the 1990s will be characterized by an even more rigid standard of population equality than those of the 1970s and 1980s.

Cases involving the redistricting of state seats followed a somewhat different path. Since Article I, Section 2 of the Constitution does not cover the state legislatures, a looser standard of population equality was pursued. After striking down the gross disparities of malapportioned districts in the 1960s, the courts seemed to point toward an informal 10 percent guideline [*Gaffney* v. *Cummings* 412 U.S. 735 (1973)]: The Court would tolerate deviations up to plus or minus 5 percent of the ideal population (i.e., a total variation of 10 percent) in order for a state legislative district to accommodate other valid reapportionment goals. However, as it did with congressional redistrictings, the Court refused to set out a clear *de minimis* standard, and this became the source of some confusion and uncertainty. In a few instances, the Supreme Court has allowed total population deviations well above the 10 percent norm. For instance, in *Mahan* v. *Howell* 410 U.S. 315 (1973), the Court sustained a plan for the Virginia legislature that closely respected local political boundaries but produced total population deviations of 16 percent, which is well above the informal 10 percent ceiling but still minuscule by historical standards. Even more dramatically, in 1983 the Court sustained a state legislative plan in Wyoming [*Brown* v. *Thomson* 426 U.S. 835

(1983)] with overall population deviations of close to 90 percent. On the other hand, in *Chapman* v. *Meier* 420 U.S. 1,95 (1975) and *Connor* v. *Finch* 431 U.S. 407 (1977), it struck down legislative districts in North Dakota and Mississippi with overall population deviations of 20 percent and less.

Whether the Court continues to be more tolerant of relatively high population differences in state legislative districts in the 1990s may depend upon how interventionist it becomes in racial and partisan vote-dilution cases. If, in the spirit of *Karcher* v. *Daggett*, it chooses to adopt an aggressive formalistic approach to gerrymandering (i.e., checking attempts to manipulate lines for political advantage by imposing rigid formal criteria), then the standards for population deviations for state legislative plans may in the future converge with the strict congressional standards. If the courts stay out of the gerrymandering issue, then line-drawers may not feel such compulsion to protect themselves by employing extremely stringent population standards.

Aside from the issue of how equal district populations should be, a second and related problem is the determination of the basis for computing district population equality. In theory, districts could be equalized with respect to total population, registered voters, actual voters, or citizens of voting age. As we will discuss later, each standard has different political implications for various groups. In general, the Court has consistently reaffirmed its preference for the Census Bureau's total population figures. However, the Court has occasionally allowed a state to use alternative data such as registration figures [e.g., Hawaii in *Burns* v. *Richardson* 384 U.S. 73 (1966)] when this does not produce a substantially different distribution of seats. But it has rejected attempts to switch the normal base from total population to one that includes only citizens or voters. The Court's reliance on total population data means that districts can have equal populations but unequal numbers of voters—especially in districts that include military bases or universities and areas that have high noncitizen populations. The importance of this will be discussed later.

A third issue arising out of the post-1962 population cases centers on which levels of government should be covered by the "one person, one vote" doctrine. There are over 80,000 units of government in the United States including the one federal and fifty state units. Does the equal population requirement pertain to county boards, city councils, special districts, schools boards, and regional governments? The Supreme Court ruled soon after *Baker* v. *Carr* that the "one person, one vote" principle did apply to local units with general governmental functions [*Avery* v. *Midland County* 390 U.S. 474 (1968)], but it declined to apply this standard to special districts that provided only very particular services such as irrigation or flood control, or in which the benefits and burden of paying for the service were unequally distributed [*Salyer Land Co.* v. *Tulare Lake Basin Water Storage District* 410 U.S. 719 (1973) and *Ball* v. *James* 451 U.S. 355 (1981)].

Some local government officials have objected that if the Court stringently applies "one person, one vote" to local governments and specialized boards, they will lose the flexibility to pursue creative local government arrangements that might promote regional cooperation or private–public partnerships for the provision of local public goods. For instance, if the San Francisco Bay area wanted to establish a new regional government to control growth or provide better transportation services, it would have to entice small cities to join with large cities. Just as in 1788, when small states worried about domination by larger states during the constitutional convention, so smaller cities worry about being subordinated to larger cities. Compromise governmental plans that give small cities equal votes with larger cities will probably violate the "one person, one vote" principle [*Board of Estimate* v. *Morris* 109 SC 1433 (1989)]. The Court's position on this issue will be watched closely in the 1990s.

Vote Dilution and Redistricting

Legal doctrine on voting rights in the post-1962 period gradually moved beyond the equal right to the franchise and the right to an equally weighted vote to a third political right—the right to a meaningful or undiluted vote. This line of reasoning holds that, even if an individual has the right to vote, and even if that vote is equally weighted, the districting arrangement can still be unequal and hence unfair. In particular, it has been argued, if the lines are drawn in such a manner as to dilute the votes of one group and enhance the electoral prospects of another, then the gains of redistricting justice brought about by the malapportionment cases can be easily nullified. The Supreme Court has had to confront this issue in two kinds of vote dilution cases—partisan (i.e., political gerrymandering) and racial (i.e., racial gerrymandering). In contrast to the Court's rapid and complete involvement in the malapportionment issue after 1962, the Court has been cautious about taking on partisan gerrymandering. Until *Davis* v. *Bandemer* 478 U.S. 109 (1986), in the few instances in which the Supreme Court actually reviewed this issue, it took an indirect approach in the spirit of *Kirkpatrick* v. *Preisler* and *Karcher* v. *Daggett*; it declined to define precisely what a partisan gerrymander was but refused to allow the violation of other constitutional criteria such as population equality for partisan purposes, even when the violations were relatively trivial.

In addition, the Supreme Court has generally been more permissive of bipartisan plans (i.e., incumbent-preserving gerrymanders) than partisan ones. In *Burns* v. *Richardson* and *White* v. *Weiser*, the Court held that drawing lines to minimize contests between sitting incumbents does not in and of itself establish "invidiousness." And in *Gaffney* v. *Cummings*, the Court went so far as to uphold a consciously political plan that attempted to create proportionate shares of districts for the two parties based on voting results in the previous three elections. In short, the Court implicitly drew a distinction in the 1970s and 1980s between political and invidiously partisan redistricting plans.

This doctrine may change in the future as the result of the important decision in *Davis* v. *Bandemer*, a case involving Indiana's state legislative districts. Indiana Democrats claimed that the district lines drawn by the Republican-controlled legislature in 1981 diluted their voting strength and resulted in disproportionate gains for Republican candidates. The Supreme Court ruled, six to three, that a political gerrymandering claim based on the equal protection clause was justiciable. However, the Court cast considerable doubt on whether this would mean anything significant in practice by overruling the lower court's decision to strike down the Indiana plan, six to three.

The plurality decision was so vaguely worded that it has been interpreted in widely different ways. Some argue that the Court meant that the evidence presented by the plaintiffs in the Indiana case was simply insufficient and that, had it been more complete, the outcome of the case would have been different. They infer from this decision that it will be necessary in future cases to show that a plan produces disproportionate results over at least two elections in order to prove a violation. Others interpret *Davis* v. *Bandemer* as suggesting that a partisan gerrymander claim will be granted only to political groups who suffer discrimination comparable to that experienced by racial minorities, and therefore that it is unlikely to apply to disputes between the two major parties. The Supreme Court's subsequent affirmation of a lower court's ruling in *Badham* v. *Eu* 109 U.S. 829 (1989), the case concerning California's 1981 redistricting, suggests that the latter prediction may prove to be correct. In this case, the federal courts refused to overturn the Democratic congressional plan, rejecting the proposition that California Republicans were in the same position of political exclusion as blacks in the South. As a consequence of these cases, the 1980s ended with considerable uncertainty over the partisan gerrymandering issue, and much litigation on this subject is bound to take place in the 1990s.

The other type of vote dilution case involves racial gerrymandering. The most significant development was the passage of the Voting Rights Act (VRA) in 1965 and the subsequent amendments to the Act, especially in 1982. While most of the VRA litigation in the 1980s involved challenges to multimember districts, Sections 2 and 5 also apply to districting arrangements. Districting in certain areas must be precleared with the Justice Department or the D.C. district court because they are covered by Section 5 of the VRA, which prevents the retrogression of voting power in areas with a history of vote discrimination and low voting participation. However, areas that are not covered by Section 5 must still meet the standards of Section 2.

Prior to the VRA's amendment in 1982, districting arrangements could be found unconstitutional only if they were intentionally drawn to dilute the votes of disadvantaged minorities [*Bolden* v. *City of Mobile* 446 U.S. 55 (1980)]. After 1982, the Act was amended by Congress so that plans that had the effect of diluting minority votes could also be overturned. In *Thornburg* v. *Gingles* 478 U.S. 30 (1986), a case involving state legislative districts in North Carolina, the Court singled out three criteria as most important in deciding whether a jurisdiction had indeed violated the Act: Is a minority group sufficiently large and compact to form a majority in a district? Is it politically cohesive? Is there evidence of racially polarized voting against it? During the 1980s, Section 2 of the VRA was applied to districting arrangements in Chicago [*Ketchum* v. *Byrne* 740 F.2d 1398 (7th Cir. 1984)], Boston (*1982–5*), Los Angeles City (*1984–5*) and Los Angeles County (*Garza* v. *County of Los Angeles*, 1989).

We will return to the problems of minority representation later. For now, it suffices to note that equality of representation in the 1980s began to evolve in new directions. Prodded by the Court's willingness to entertain political gerrymandering cases and by the newly amended provisions of the VRA, states must now think about representational equality in new terms. These new terms include the right to fair electoral outcomes, as opposed to simply the equal right to participate, and rights of people in groups (i.e., as Democrats, Republicans, blacks, Latinos, etc.), as opposed to the rights of individuals alone.

Politics in the Post-1962 Period— No End to Controversy

Redistricting in the seventies was by recent standards relatively noncontroversial. Most states were able to complete their congressional redistrictings within the period between January 1971 and the summer of 1982. One exception was California, where the lines drawn by the Democratic legislature in 1971 were vetoed by Governor Reagan. The task of drawing new lines was postponed until the next session, but even then the legislature was unable to break the deadlock and devise a compromise. In May 1973, when the legislature passed a second redistricting bill, the governor vetoed it as well. The state supreme court was forced to appoint the Masters (three retired justices) and staff, and they proceeded to draw up a plan in November 1973.

In addition to California, the courts were drawn into the redistricting of six other states—Connecticut, Michigan, Mississippi, Illinois, New Jersey, and Washington. Most states, however, were able to do the job themselves, and most of these did it in a bipartisan manner. Consensus was probably facilitated in 1971 by the fact that this round of redistricting occurred so soon after the post-*Baker* v. *Carr* adjustments of the mid-1960s, which meant that the old district lines needed relatively small and uncontroversial changes to meet constitutional standards.

Only a handful of states had partisan disputes—Florida, Oklahoma, Arizona, Colorado, and New York. For instance, Republicans in Florida complained that the Democrats designed their districts to preserve the existing nine-to-three advantage they enjoyed and to gain two of the state's three new districts, strengthening marginal Democratic seats and weakening marginal Republican ones. In turn, Republicans were accused of eliminating two inner-city Democratic seats in New York and gaining the advantage in new seats in Colorado and Arizona.

The drift to the sunbelt was markedly reflected in the apportionment of congressional districts **across** the states (see Table 2.2). But the net effect of the 1971 redistrictings upon the various interests **within** the states was less clear. The urban-rural imbalance had been primarily redressed in the mid-1960s round of redistrictings so that the effect of additional changes in this regard was relatively marginal. There was, however, a slight partisan shift in congressional party balance. According to one estimate, 18 seats went into Republican hands as the result of the 1971 redrawing, and 8 went to the Democrats—a net Republican gain of 10 (*Congressional Quarterly*, 1985).

Some Republicans felt that the gains might have been marginally greater if the courts had given them better districting plans in those states where the courts drew the boundaries. This was especially true in California where the lines adopted by the appointed Masters appeared to many to be very similar to the Democratic legislature's plan (and perhaps even more favorable to the Democrats).

In most states, however, the perception of court bias seemed to be greatest when it adopted lines drawn by outside parties. For instance, Republicans were unhappy when the courts in Michigan, Connecticut, and Missouri all accepted plans submitted to them by Democrats.

With the experience of two previous redistrictings to rely upon and knowing that the option of doing nothing in order to avoid controversy was foreclosed, political groups approached the 1981 redistricting with much greater preparation and anticipation than in 1971. The Republicans made a special effort to gain control of more state legislatures in the late 1970s in order to have an increased voice in the redistricting process. They also moved more quickly than the Democrats to embrace the new computer technology that would allow them to assess the political impact of various proposals with less difficulty and higher accuracy. Republican-leaning institutions such as the Rose Institute made their information and services available to minority groups, hoping that the prospect of more heavily minority-dominated districts would cause the weakening of white Democratic incumbent seats and cause more court challenges to Democratic redistricting plans.

The previous decade of litigation over racial vote dilution had sensitized black and Latino groups to the importance of the way in which district lines were drawn and made them much more willing to lobby for their interests. In addition, at the local level, because a number of communities had abandoned controversial at-large and multimember systems and converted to single-member systems, there were more district lines to be drawn than before.

Indeed, there was controversy even before the first lines were drawn in 1981. Black and Latino spokesmen, as well as many city government officials, voiced their concern about the possibility of a census undercount. The 1970 census had missed 2.5 percent of the population. The error was particularly great in minority communities. By the Census Bureau's own estimates, they missed 7.7 percent of blacks as compared to 1.9 percent of whites. Cities with large minority populations, such as New York, feared that the undercount would cost them their rightful share of political representation and reduce federal money allotted to them. The city of Detroit filed suit against the federal government seeking an upward revision in the

Census Bureau's numbers to reflect the undercount of minorities. The district court ruled for the plaintiffs but was overruled by the 6th U.S. Circuit Court of Appeals on the grounds that the claim was a hypothetical one based on the 1970 experience.

As in 1971, the political shift resulting from a new apportionment in 1981 was to distribute seats from the Northeast and Midwest to the fast-growing sunbelt region and from the inner cities to the suburbs. This time, Florida gained four new seats; Texas three; California two; and Arizona, Colorado, Nevada, New Mexico, Oregon, Tennessee, Utah, and Washington one each. By contrast, New York lost five seats; Illinois and Pennsylvania two each; and Indiana, Massachusetts, Michigan, Missouri, New Jersey, and South Dakota one each.

With 17 seats shifting across states, the heightened expectations of so many groups, and a decade elapsing between redistrictings, it is not surprising that the 1981 revisions took longer than those in 1971 and that they caused more political controversy. Only 25 of the 44 states with more than one congressional seat completed their redistricting by January 1982 (*Congressional Quarterly*, 1985).

Although most redistrictings were bipartisan in 1981, there were several well-publicized and acrimonious partisan redistrictings. In Indiana, the Republicans concentrated the voting strength of the Democrats in a manner that gave them a better chance at winning three of the six seats the Democrats held. In California, the legislature gave the redistricting task over to Congressman Phil Burton, and he reconfigured the lines in a manner that altered the Democratic advantage from 22–21 to 28–17. The Republicans placed the legislature's redistricting bills on the 1982 ballot as referendum issues, but the state supreme court ruled that those lines could be used for the 1982 election. The "no" vote prevailed in the referendum, and the legislature redrew its districts after the election but before the new Republican governor came into office.

Looking back over the nearly thirty years following the *Baker v. Carr* decision, it is clear that the Court's decisions have not lessened the controversy of redistricting. The increasingly strict application of "one person, one vote" may have taken away a powerful political tool, malapportionment, but other redistricting concerns are as intense as ever.

The form of those concerns, however, has changed a great deal. In the 1950s and 1960s, rural versus urban power was the critical cleavage underlying the reapportionment debate. Resistance to the doctrine of "one person, one vote" was strongest in rural communities and counties that enjoyed disproportionate power under the old arrangements. As we shall see later, considerations such as respecting county lines or constructing districts that preserve rural communities of interest are by no means completely dead, but in most states the intensity of the rural versus urban redistricting issue had waned considerably by the 1980s.

Racial and ethnic redistricting issues, on the other hand, are far more salient now than they were in the 1950s. Partly, this is because the population in many urban areas has become more diverse, particularly where there has been a great deal of immigration from Mexico, Latin America, and Asia. Partly, it is because of the Voting Rights Act of 1965, especially after it was amended in 1982; states and localities that draw lines without regard for the contours of black and Latino neighborhoods risk being challenged in court. And partly, it is because many racial and ethnic minorities have learned from past experiences that redistricting matters and that they must exert political pressure upon the system if they are going to secure additional gains for their communities.

Conclusion

It is clear from our brief review of redistricting history that the so-called reapportionment revolution is at a critical crossroads. Each step in the Court's intervention into redistricting has led logically to a next further step. The goal of an equally weighted vote was initially directed against gross malapportionment, but later extended to relatively small variations from the ideal population at practically all levels of government. But groups could still gain advantages by manipulating boundary lines even under the constraint of the equal population requirement. If the right of each person's vote were to be made truly equal, then perhaps the courts had to do more, or so it seemed to some. The right to an equally weighted vote led to the right to an undiluted vote.

But the transition from the former to the latter was significant and controversial. What exactly is a diluted vote? Is everyone protected from vote dilution or are only disadvantaged racial and ethnic minority groups protected? The courts' decisions in these areas during the 1980s raised as many questions as they answered. Opponents of the idea that the courts had jurisdiction in this area warned that there was no natural stopping point and that the courts would get sucked into the mire of partisan politics. Court decisions in the next decade will reveal whether the critics predicted the future correctly.

C H A P T E R 3

BUILDING BLOCKS

Politics is the stuff of redistricting controversy, but drawing new district boundaries also involves complicated technical questions. The raw data of population and geography have to be processed into manageable form before arguments over principles or politics can commence. Thus, at one level, redistricting is about political posturing, bargaining, and negotiation, but at another, it is about population data, computers, statistics, and census maps. This unusual combination of convoluted politics and esoteric technical issues makes redistricting the quintessential insiders' game—a game that is hard for outsiders to follow and even harder, if not impossible, for them to play.

At the other end of the spectrum is a breed of congressional incumbents and political consultants who learn to master and even relish the arcane aspects of this exercise. The late California Congressman Phil Burton built much of his reputation as a political mastermind on his formidable redistricting expertise. Burton boasted that he knew the political landscape of the state's congressional districts better than the incumbents who represented them, right down to the exact location of low-turnout trailer parks and high-turnout senior citizen homes. Much of this knowledge was stored in his head. In an era when computers and large data sets are regarded as essential redistricting tools, Burton did all his work in 1981 on a pocket calculator and persuaded the legislature to pass his plan without ever producing a detailed set of maps of the new districts.

On the surface, the technical task of redistricting appears to be the same in all states: The boundaries of congressional districts must be adjusted so that the populations in all of them are equal. The

42

actual technical demands, however, vary greatly. In states with small populations and more than one congressional seat, the software and hardware requirements are nonexistent or relatively minor, involving small numbers of census tracts and little or no computational complexity. However, in large states such as California, New York, and Texas, redistricting is a major technical challenge. It is no simple matter to manipulate an enormous amount of census and political data in the short period of time between the census and the next congressional election.

This chapter will deal with the basic materials and technical processes of redistricting. What are the key steps in drawing new congressional boundaries? How are the census and political data used? How are critical redistricting parameters measured? The next chapter will then uncover the political choices embedded in the technical tasks of drawing new district boundaries.

The Phases of Congressional Redistricting

As we noted in the last chapter, the task of drawing new congressional district boundaries occurs in two phases. The first is the apportionment of congressional seats to the fifty states, and the second is the adjustment of congressional district boundaries within the states after the initial state allocation has taken place. The decennial census has provided the trigger for congressional redistricting and, with the exception of 1920, it has always been followed by a reallocation of congressional seats between the states. In addition to the federal constitutional mandate to redistrict after a census, some state constitutions also explicitly require that their state legislatures be redistricted every ten years. In some states, it is possible not only to redistrict too infrequently, but also to redistrict too often. A California state court ruled in 1984 that a ballot proposition called the Sebastiani Initiative, which would have redrawn congressional boundaries for a second time after the 1980 census, violated the one redistricting per decade provision of the California constitution.

Since 1962, the Court's "one person, one vote" rulings have further regularized the redistricting timetable so that almost all levels of government down to the local school districts are on a ten-year cycle. But this practice is not standard internationally. New Zealand draws its boundaries every five years, Australia every seven years, and Britain every fifteen years, while India and France have allowed over twenty years to elapse without a change. The actual responsibility for counting the population in the United States has been delegated by Congress to the Department of Commerce and its Bureau of the Census. The Census Bureau is directed by law to make its national enumeration as of April 1 in the first year of a decade (i.e., 1970, 1980, 1990, etc.) and to complete it in nine months, reporting the results to the president by December 31 of the census year. The number of representatives each state receives is based on the new census figures as determined by a proportional population calculation. More specifically, each state, no matter how small, is first allocated one congressional seat, and then the remaining 385 seats are apportioned by the "method of equal proportions" formula (which ranks the state's priority of seat assignment by population adjusted by the number of seats already allocated to it).

The first phase of reapportionment is the most purely mechanical part of the process. Once state populations have been determined and announced by the Census Bureau, the method of equal proportions formula neutrally assigns each state its proper share of seats. The fact that Phase 1 is highly mechanical, however, does not mean that it is uncontroversial. As we discussed earlier, there has been much disagreement over how best to calculate the proportional allocation formula since differences in methods of calculation can affect the exact allocation of the last few seats.

The quality of the census can also be an important issue at this stage. If a state believes that it has been disproportionately undercounted and if it has just narrowly lost out on acquiring another congressional seat, variations in the final census figures can affect Phase 1 politics. However, the apportionment phase is apolitical in the sense that outcomes are not influenced by the party that controls Congress or by incumbents protecting their own best interests.

The second phase of congressional redistricting is the adjustment of seat boundaries within the states. Once a state's share of congressional seats has been determined, the boundaries of any new seats along with the old ones must be fixed so as to produce equal populations among all the state's congressional districts. For this purpose, the commerce secretary is required by law to hand over to the states by April 1 of the year after the census was taken population counts at the census tract and census block level. In this narrow sense, the second phase, like the first, is a form of apportionment, because congressional districts are being apportioned to cities and counties within a state after they are apportioned to the different states.

However, there are some critical differences between these two phases. Seats in the first phase are apportioned to states by a strictly neutral formula, but in the second they are apportioned to cities and counties by negotiation within a commission or the state legislature. The second phase, in short, is a much more political process than the first. Another difference is that states have congressional districts wholly contained within their boundaries and share no parts of a district with other states, whereas congressional districts can contain those parts of cities and counties needed to make the ideal population. Seats, in other words, can only be wholly apportioned to states, but can be either wholly or partially apportioned to cities and counties.

A critical aspect of the second phase of the redistricting cycle is the limited timetable in which states must finish their tasks. In large states especially, a complex process has to be done at high speed. The Census Bureau is under a great deal of pressure to complete the gargantuan job of counting every person in the United States and giving the data to the states by April 1 of the year after the census (e.g., 1991). The legal dates of primary races and the statutory filing requirements make it essential that the new districts should be firmly delineated by autumn of that year. This results in a good deal of frantic bargaining and hasty court appeals and, not surprisingly, some states fail to make their deadlines.

When deadlines are not met, the courts are faced with a number of equally unsavory options. If elections are held in the old district lines and there are significant population imbalances, then the rights of individual voters will be violated. But if the courts allow candidates to run at-large until the final district lines are determined, this could result in a voting rights violation in states with large numbers of racial and ethnic minority voters (for the same reason that at-large electoral mechanisms have been challenged under the VRA). Or finally, the courts can draw their own lines or choose between alternative plans submitted to them, but by so doing, they risk partisan and political criticism on the part of unhappy factions and parties. Since neither the state legislatures nor the courts themselves prefer giving the task over to the judiciary, the incentives to avoid legislative deadlock over redistricting are considerable. In contrast with the hurried schedule of U.S. redistricting, most other countries work with a more flexible timetable. For instance, the English Boundary Commission started work in 1976, but it was not until 1983 that its recommendations (based on the 1976 electoral register) passed into law. The only virtue of such dilatoriness is that it allowed ample time for detailed quasi-judicial enquiries into the merits of different proposals. But a commission system can also work swiftly, observing all due process, as Australia showed in 1984 when, in a mere seven months, 125 constituencies were comprehensively redrawn into 148 new areas.

A Hypothetical Illustration

To illustrate what occurs in the second stage of congressional redistricting, consider the following highly simplified example. Let us assume that a state has been informed on December 31 of the census year that it will get to keep its four congressional districts. As a result of population changes over the last decade, this imaginary state finds itself with a population of 400 distributed over the four seats as follows (see Figure 3.1).

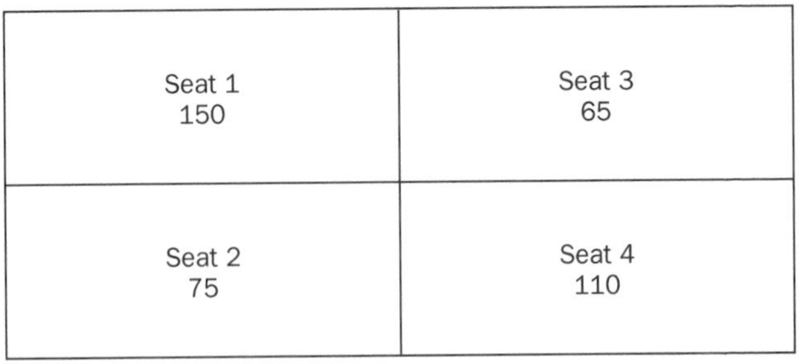

Seat 1 150	Seat 3 65
Seat 2 75	Seat 4 110

Figure 3.1 Hypothetical example of unbalanced seat populations.

The ideal quota is the number of people that must be contained in each district if each is to be equally populated. This quota is arrived at by dividing the state's population (i.e., 400) by the number of congressional seats that it has been given (i.e., 4). The ideal population in this hypothetical example is therefore 100. By this standard, some of the districts have too much population and some have too little. The difference between the district population and the ideal population is called the absolute deviation. The absolute deviations for the seats in this example are Seat 1: +50, Seat 2: −25, Seat 3: −35, Seat 4: +10.

When the Court considers whether a population discrepancy is acceptable or unacceptable, it frequently looks at the relative deviation—the absolute deviation divided by the ideal population. The rule of thumb for congressional seats, which we discussed earlier, is that districts must not vary in relative deviation by more or less than 1 percent. All of the districts in our example violate this standard by a considerable degree (50 percent in Seat 1, 25 percent in Seat 2, 35 percent in Seat 3, and 10 percent in Seat 4).

The Court will also refer to such terms as the mean deviation (the average of all the relative deviations—in this case 30 percent), the relative range of deviation (from 50 percent to −35 percent in our example) and the overall range of deviation (85 percent). Using these technical terms, we can restate the purpose of the second phase of congressional redistricting as reducing the relative deviation in any given seat to as close to zero as is possible and the overall range in all the seats to less than 1 percent at a maximum. However, there are no guarantees in this exercise, because the Court has refused to set out hard and fast minimal standards. The real goal of congressional redistricting, then, lies in achieving overall deviations that are as close to zero as possible, because the Court might regard any deviation more than zero, no matter how minute, as constitutionally unacceptable.

As a practical matter, the population deviations in our hypothetical example can be reduced in a number of ways. This is illustrated in Figure 3.2. For instance, Seat 1 could give 25 constituents to Seat 2 and 25 to Seat 3, while Seat 4 gives 10 to Seat 3. Alternatively, Seat 1 could give 50 to Seat 3; Seat 3, 15 to Seat 4; and Seat 4, 25 to Seat 2. But there's the rub. Since there are usually many ways to

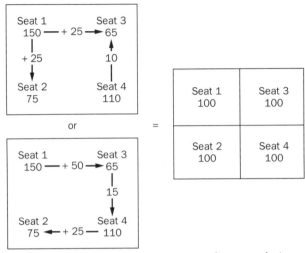

Figure 3.2   Alternative ways to equalize populations.

satisfy the basic task of making the districts equipopulous, and since each of them will inevitably lead to different political, racial, and regional consequences, people can always disagree about the best way to reapportion the districts in a state.

The situation becomes more complex if we add some plausible wrinkles (see Figures 3.3 and 3.4). Let us assume that our hypothetical state has been apportioned a fifth seat by the federal formula. The ideal population is now 80, and the state must not only decide how to deal with its overpopulated existing districts, but where to place its new district. The first step in congressional redistricting thus affects the difficulty and nature of the task in the second step. States that have to add or subtract a district from their delegations first have to make decisions about where to place their new districts or remove old ones before they can adjust the populations of their remaining congressional seats.

Returning to our example, if we need to add a new seat, we might decide to put it in the area of the most overpopulated district, Seat 1. Seat 1 is thus divided into Seat 1 with 80 and Seat 5 with 70. Seat 5 still needs to pick up 10, which it might do from Seat 3. Seat 2

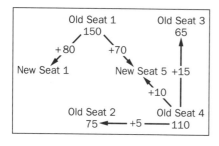

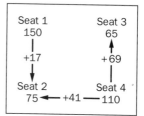

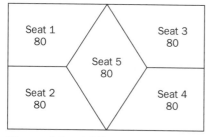

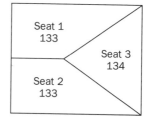

Figure 3.3 Adding a new
congressional district.

Figure 3.4 Dropping
a congressional district.

might then pick up 5 from Seat 4, and Seat 3 makes up its deficit
of 25 from Seat 4 also. In this case, all the hypothetical incumbents
except one (i.e., the representative of Seat 2) are losing a significant
number of constituents they had represented for all or part of the
last decade. The number of constituents added to or subtracted
from a seat is referred to as displacement. As this example shows, a
change in one seat can affect the amount of displacement suffered by
another. If the 10 needed by Seat 5 are taken from Seat 2 rather than
Seat 3, then the burden of displacement has been shifted accordingly.
With a larger number of districts, the cascading or rippling effects
of population changes from a district in one part of the state upon
another are even more complicated.

The same sorts of problems arise when the state's representation must be reduced. If the allocation formula dictates that our
hypothetical state must drop a seat, from four to three, the ideal
population becomes 133.3. While the powers of the reapportioner

are considerable, they do not as yet include dividing people into fractions—there is no known way to draw districts which have 133.3 people in them. Thus of mathematical necessity, one district will have a larger population than the other two, a point worth remembering when we later consider the Court's quest for strict population equality.

One logical way to proceed toward this goal is to abolish Seat 3 and merge it into Seat 4. Seat 2 can make up its deficit by acquiring 17 from Seat 1 and 41 from Seat 4. This of course often means that two or more incumbents may be running for the newly enlarged Seat 4, and as we shall see later, this inevitably results in bitter political fighting.

One side issue that arises most often in situations when seats are added to or taken from a state's delegation is the assignment of a number to a congressional seat. In some countries, constituencies are given names, not numbers, and controversies can arise over which of the component towns should provide the label for the seat. In Australia, many districts are named after famous political figures, and this has sometimes caused political resentment.

In the United States, however, the practice of numbering congressional districts has survived unchallenged since 1790, but even this can cause trouble when an incumbent finds that redistricting has changed the numbering of his seat. For instance, in our hypothetical example, the incumbent in District 1 would want to keep the number 1 for his new district if the old district were divided into two parts so that he could continue to be listed as the incumbent on the ballot. However, the advantage of having the same number is not as important as that of retaining as much of his or her former district as possible (i.e., minimal displacement) or having one's residence remain inside the district.

Numbering issues are more important in state and local electoral systems when terms are staggered and linked to the district's number. For instance, if upper house districts in state legislatures with even numbers are scheduled to run in the first election after the redistricting (e.g., 1982, 1992), then an incumbent with an even numbered district can get an extra two years without running by switching his district to an odd number. By the reverse logic, an unpopular incumbent or one in a marginal district can be forced to run earlier than otherwise by changing the number from odd to even. Since all congressional seats are up for election every two years, odd versus even numbering is not an important issue at the federal level.

So far, our examples have been very unrealistic in an important sense—namely, that district population changes are actually made by moving around discrete population chunks called census tracts and census blocks rather than individuals *per se*. For instance, in the simplest case discussed above—adjusting the four districts so that each has a population of 100—we suggested that one way of achieving this was to move 25 people from Seat 1 with its surplus of 50 to Seat 2 with its deficit of 25. We could do this by moving a whole census tract from district A to district B, but it would be extremely fortuitous if there were a tract with exactly the right number of people in it. More frequently, the tracts will be just a little larger or smaller than the number one needs.

This is illustrated by dividing our hypothetical districts into census tracts (see Figure 3.5). Since census tracts 3 and 4 lie on the border between Seats 1 and 2, the logical way to adjust the population imbalance between the two is to move one of those tracts into Seat 2. However, to add census tract 3 to Seat 2 would raise its population to 136, switching from a deficit of 25 to a surplus of

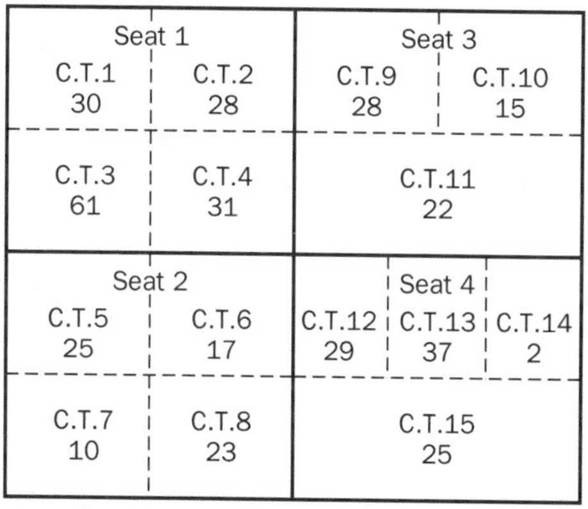

Figure 3.5 Working with the census tracts.

36. Adding tract 4 gets us closer to population equality, but we still produce a surplus of 6 for Seat 2 as well as 6 fewer to transfer to Seat 3, which needs to acquire 25 from Seat 1 also. In short, transferring census tract 4 from Seat 1 to Seat 2 would bring us closer to population equality but still would not produce the exact equality that the Court is looking for.

Fortunately, the Census Bureau provides subunits of census tracts called census blocks. Where the tracts are composed of thousands of people, the blocks are typically composed of hundreds of people. In our simplified example, the problem of population imbalance is solved if one of the blocks inside census tract 4 has a population of 6 and is contiguous to census tracts 1, 2, or 3 (see Figure 3.6). Since, in our example, block 1 in census tract 4 is next

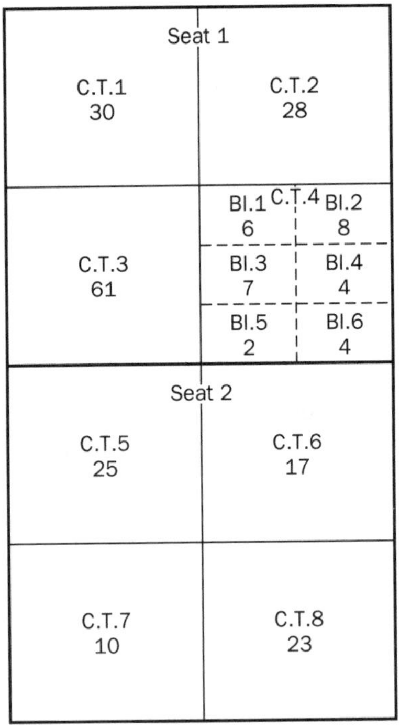

Figure 3.6 Importance of census block configurations.

to census tracts 1, 2, and 3, we can place all the other blocks into Seat 2 and leave block 1 in Seat 1 and achieve population equality in Seat 2. Needless to say, we will not be so lucky most of the time. Often, none of the blocks has precisely the right population, or when one does, it can lie in a geographically awkward position. If, for instance, block 4 has the population of 6 instead of block 1 and we put the rest of the blocks into Seat 2, block 4 would no longer be contiguous to any portion of Seat 1.

The quest for finer refinements in population equality can lead to complicated trades between districts. If there is no combination of blocks in census tract 4 that achieves perfect equality, then we might move census tract 4 into Seat 2 and then try to find blocks in census tract 3 on the border between Seats 1 and 2 or blocks in census tract 9 in Seat 3 that could be added to compensate for the imbalance created by not breaking up census tract 4. This highlights once again the interdependence of redistricting trades between different seats— a population need in one area can cause a previously unforeseen change in another area. One option that is foreclosed is dividing the census blocks. Since the census block is the smallest unit made available by the Census Bureau on its redistricting database tape, a census block unit cannot be divided without risking a challenge and possible reversal by the courts.

As this hypothetical example illustrates, redistricting works with discrete chunks of population. As a consequence, many complicated trades are needed as reapportioners try to find the combination of census tract and block changes that gets closest to the goal of exact population equality for all districts. It also means that in most instances it will be impossible to achieve precise equality because the units being shifted are too coarse.

The Data for Redistricting

Redistricting, especially if it is to achieve equal sized constituencies, should be based on reliable statistics. Are the data accurate? The United States has always made population, as determined by the Census Bureau, the basis for the allocation of seats. From 1790 to 1870 slaves were counted as three-fifths of a person, and American Indians not paying taxes were excluded. While the three-fifths provision disappeared in 1870, the precedent for using population (including most categories of nonvoters) lingers to this day. Retaining the tradition of basing redistricting upon population in a census area rather than lists of voters or voting age eligible population means that noncitizens, felons, and children are counted for apportionment purposes even though they are not eligible to vote. Since 1970, military personnel stationed at a base and students in local universities have also been included in the enumeration of a census tract.

Britain and some other countries with compulsory electoral registration (i.e., where the state is required to compile registration rolls of eligible persons) have preferred to use the number of qualified voters; this eliminates foreigners and children from the calculation, although it can be argued that these categories deserve representation quite as much as native-born or naturalized adults.

However, even if it is accepted that population rather than voters should provide the quotas for calculating representation, the census figures do not always provide a secure basis for the allocation of seats. Censuses are fallible, and the degree to which their figures offer a complete count of the population vary from area to area. The Census Bureau estimates that it counted 99 percent of the white population in 1980 but only 94 percent of the African-Americans. Many fear that the problem has become even greater in the last decade.

The Census Bureau collects its numbers in two stages. The first is a mail-in questionnaire, and the second is a follow-up enumeration of those who fail to return their forms. In 1980, the response rate for the mail-in forms was 75 percent, and the target response for 1990 was 70 percent. Instead, the Bureau received only 63 percent of the forms it sent out. The low response rate required enumerators to visit an additional 35 million households at an expense of close to seventy million dollars. Given the rising number of homeless, the severe danger of violence in many low-income, nonwhite neighborhoods, and the large number of undocumented aliens crowded into substandard and unconventional housing arrangements (e.g., living in garages, back apartments, or tool sheds), it seemed implausible to census critics that the disadvantaged inner-city areas were being properly counted. There were over 50 lawsuits challenging the 1980 census, and a majority of them focused on undercount problems. Other lawsuits challenged the inclusion of undocumented aliens and overseas citizens in the figures used for redistricting.

Challenges to the 1990 census began early. In 1987, the Census Bureau announced that there would be no postenumeration adjustment to the 1990 census. A number of cities sought to enjoin the Bureau from taking the census, and as part of the settlement, the Census Bureau was forced to keep the option of adjustments before the release and after preliminary review by local governments alive until July 15, 1991. The Census Bureau was anxious to ensure that any adjustment in the count did not delay or tie up the progress of redistricting. On the other hand, by its own admission, the 1990 census probably missed between 4 and 6 million people. Controversy over undercount and the need for adjustment could lead to prolonged rounds of litigation in the early 1990s.

In addition to the accuracy of the count, there are other important census issues. One of these, for instance, concerns the demographic groups which are given separate designations on the census form. If particular racial or ethnic groups want to ensure that district lines at all levels incorporate rather than divide their neighborhoods, it is essential that redistricters have a proper count of their numbers. If the Census Bureau does not provide a separate category for a particular racial or ethnic group, this seriously diminishes the chances of a beneficial redistricting. Census data about the sizes and locations of minority groups are also critical pieces of evidence in voting rights litigation if and when district lines are later challenged. Thus, Latinos lobbied for a separate census category in 1980, and Asian-Americans fought off attempts in 1988 to reduce the eleven different Asian–Pacific Island categories into a single one.

Another issue with using the census figures as the basis of redistricting is that the numbers can become inaccurate over time. Census data, even when accurate for the moment of enumeration, can be rapidly made obsolete by the movements of population. It is worth pointing out that in Australia, with its seven-year redistribution of seats, the Electoral Commission is required to work not from current figures but from the census projections of what the population of each locality will be in three-and-a-half years' time. In the United States, however, the Court has looked very skeptically at redistrictings based on any numbers other than the census enumeration. A state that used projections of population a year or two after the census, or that purposely gave some districts substantially less than average population in order to allow for projected growth in the future, would open itself up to legal challenge, particularly if by using the alternative data or allowing for higher population deviations it produced a plan that was substantially different from one that would have been produced using the census figures. In effect, the Court can only guarantee "one person, one vote" at the time of the census and not throughout the decade.

A last problem, and one which is partly behind the legal challenge to counting aliens and overseas citizens for redistricting purposes, is that equality of census population does not produce equality of voters. Even if all constituencies were to contain equal population, the electorates would not be equal. That is because the proportion of nonvoters is not uniform across the population. The proportion too young to vote in 1980 ranged between districts from 5 percent to 35 percent. The proportion of noncitizens, officially 3 percent of the population, ranged from almost nothing to over 10 percent—or perhaps more in urban centers where illegal immigrants congregate. Even among adult citizens the propensity to register varies greatly; so, too, does the proportion of those registered who cast their votes.

Thus perfect equality in numbers can never be achieved for these obvious reasons: census errors, differences in the age and citizenship of subpopulations, uneven rates of growth during the following decade, and variations in political participation. Consider the districts shown in Table 3.1. In these four examples—all of them equipopulous congressional districts—the proportion of voting age population varies from 63 percent to 81 percent. The change in population between 1980 and 1986 varies from a decrease of 6 percent to an increase of 33 percent. The proportion voting varies from 11 percent to 37 percent. Clearly the static and broad-based nature of the census data limits the degree to which the Court can really guarantee "one person, one vote."

Table 3.1 Examples of Population and Vote Discrepancies

District	Population 1986 (000s)	Population 1980 (000s)	Percentage Change 1980–1986	VAP[a] 1980	As Percentage of VAP Population	Votes Cast 1982 (000s)	As Percentage of VAP 1980
N.Y. 17th	550	516	+7	442	86	123	23
N.Y. 18th	485	517	−7	327	63	57	11
Fla. 11th	683	512	+33	380	74	154	30
Ore. 4th	509	526	−3	379	74	196	37

[a]Voting age population.

Political Data

In addition to census data, redistricting usually requires political data. The census figures can tell a great deal about the socioeconomic characteristics at the census tract or block level. Supplementing the initial April redistricting data—which only contains information about total population, voting age population, race, gender, and ethnicity—the Census Bureau later issues a more complete census report with figures on income, education, home ownership, and the like. But even the expanded version of the census data does not give a very complete profile of a district's politics. For this purpose, most states will add party registration data (if it is available) and returns from previous statewide and local races.

Party registration data are the precinct-level figures for the percent registered as Democrats, Republicans, minor parties, and independents. If the precinct-level registration data is properly matched to the census database, it is possible to monitor how various changes in district composition would affect the relative support for various parties. In the past, matching census with political data was very difficult in many states, because precinct lines were rarely designed along census tract or block lines. As a consequence, the compilation of redistricting data sets was a very expensive proposition, and in the end, because the political data had to be approximated, it was not completely accurate. In 1990, all the states participated in a program that furnished the Census Bureau with maps of precinct lines in advance of the enumeration, so that the demographic data could be provided by precinct. States then had the option of working with precincts as opposed to census tracts and blocks when they drew new districts. In addition to more reliable political data, the states hoped to minimize the amount of reprecincting they would have to do after their redistrictings: If states work with the precinct units rather than census units, they are less likely to split old precinct lines, which forces registrars to redraw new precincts.

Many states do not record party registration data. Another way to get a measure of baseline strength is to find a proxy for a so-called normal vote in a given area. One way to do this is to use one or more statewide races that seem to follow a normal pattern of partisanship. Often statewide constitutional offices are good for this purpose—the lieutenant governor, attorney general, secretary of state, or state treasurer. Taking the average of several of these or simply one good race, it is possible to monitor how the outcome would change if the district boundaries were altered. Other kinds of races can also provide useful information. A contest in which a party's candidate fared very poorly makes a good loyalty measure, since it reveals how large the most loyal component of a party's following is. For instance, Jimmy Carter's 1980 and Walter Mondale's 1984 presidential races, in white suburban areas especially, offer good loyalty tests. A Democratic incumbent whose 1980 Carter and 1984 Mondale scores go up after the district lines are changed can rest assured that he or she has been given a safer seat. Incumbents will also want to look at returns from their previous races although, of course, that information is useless in assessing areas the incumbent might acquire but has never run in before. It does, however, reveal something about the areas that might be lost in proposed redistricting trades. Minority incumbents will often take an interest in statewide races involving candidates from their own racial or ethnic group. When compared to the party registration in a given area, this data warns them of party supporters who might not vote for black and Latino candidates.

A major consumer of political information is the incumbent. While congressional incumbents do not get to vote on their own lines, they are usually consulted about their reactions to different proposals and are sometimes given a say in drawing up the lines. However, political information is also important to others. The courts use political information to assess voting rights claims brought by racial and ethnic minorities. They are particularly interested in evidence of political cohesion among a plaintiff group (e.g., do blacks or Latinos vote as a block, and can they claim to be a cohesive political group?) and in racial polarization (e.g., do white voters tend to vote against nonwhite candidates?). Political gerrymandering claims also require political data. Plaintiffs must show among other things that there is a systematic pattern of partisan underrepresentation over a series of elections as a consequence of redistricting, and this requires political returns from congressional races.

All of this political and demographic information makes redistricting a highly quantitative exercise. A typical system in a large state stores this information on a tape or disk in a computer. Usually redistricters only work with a subset of the data—population, racial and ethnic percentages, and a few critical political measures. The rest of the information is retrieved and presented when requested by the courts, or incumbents, or the press. The most advanced systems are interactive. The redistricter signifies to the computer a desire to move a particular census unit or precinct out of one district and into another, and the computer instantaneously retabulates the summary of political and demographic information after the change. The computer system must also have the capacity to provide a detailed description of the districts in terms of tracts and blocks so that the proposal can be made into a law.

Maps and Measures of Compactness

A modern redistricting computer system will have a mapping capacity so that people can view what is happening under different proposals. There are two basic kinds of maps. One is a computerized map which shows the whole county down to the census block or precinct level. An innovation of the 1990 census has been the creation of the so-called TIGER file system which adds various prominent geographic features, such as roads and railroad tracks to the computer map. However, even with these additional features, most people find the computer-generated maps hard to read and too sparse. Often people will want very specific information about side streets, neighborhoods, and topography which require a finer grade of map.

The second type of map is the printed precinct or census maps providing extremely detailed information about streets and other features. The advantage of the first type of map is that the computer can automatically and instantaneously generate a new map with each proposal. The drawback, as we said before, is its sparseness. The advantage of the second type of map is the richness of the information it provides, but a very serious limitation is the difficulty in generating them after even minor changes are made. When highly detailed maps are not on the computer, districts must be drawn in by hand, and in a large state with thousands of census tracts, delays and mistakes are inevitable.

Maps provide several essential pieces of information. For incumbents, they show in visual form the areas that have been lost and gained in a redistricting trade. Using the census and political information, a map can be colored or shaded to reflect the partisan strength or racial and ethnic composition of various areas within a proposed district. The maps are also important for displaying "holes"—parts of districts that are noncontiguous. In the mad rush to construct numerous proposals in a short period of time, it is easy to forget to assign a tract in the middle of the district or to mistakenly type in the wrong tract or block number. Mapping the districts shows these mistakes and allows for rapid correction.

A third use of maps is to assess the shapes of districts. For reasons we will discuss more fully in the next chapter, it may be important to measure the compactness of proposed districts and to compute the average compactness of districts in one proposal as opposed to the average in another. An element of compactness that has been mentioned already is contiguity—that all parts of a district must be connected at a point. Generally, it is further taken to mean connected at some point on dry land, but not always. Phil Burton claimed contiguity for a district in his 1981 California congressional plan that ran from Marin County across the waters of San Francisco Bay to the city of Vallejo. Another district in Los Angeles county followed the coastline and dock areas of Long Beach and San Pedro so narrowly that it was said of the district that it was contiguous at low tide only. Of course, some kinds of noncontiguity are unavoidable. An off-shore island, for instance, has to be attached to mainland districts by water unless it has, by itself, close to the ideal population for a district.

The other aspect of compactness is that districts should have relatively geometrical shapes, without many branches, dips, or jagged edges. A compactness requirement tries to limit oddly shaped districts, and a compactness measure provides a means for calibrating how closely districts come to meeting that goal. There are two basic forms of compactness requirements, apart from the informal eyeball reaction that people have to what they see. The first is area based and the second is population based.

An area-based measure is concerned only with the shape of a district (Young, 1988). There are a number of ways of defining such a criterion. Certain irregular shapes will pass the compactness test if one kind of measure is used but fail if another is used instead, and vice versa. For instance, a common form of an area compactness criterion is a perimeter test. One such test is to draw two concentric circles, the first wholly containing every part of a district and the second wholly contained within the district; a reasonably compact district is one in which the area of the second circle is at least 50 percent that of the first. Figure 3.7a shows a rectangular shaped

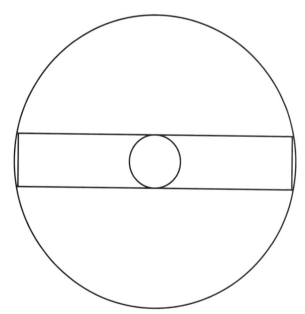

Figure 3.7a Rectangle fails perimeter/area-based compactness.

district that fails this test. However, Figure 3.7b shows a district with a number of dips and jagged edges that passes the concentric circles test and yet would seem intuitively to be noncompact. A smallest square criterion, by comparison, does a better job of catching jagged edges, but not smooth, rectangular forms.

Another less frequently employed compactness measure is population based. The intuition behind this is that compactness is important only where there are people: Oddly shaped lines that are caused by natural features (e.g., the contours of the coast or a mountain range) should not be judged in the same way as oddly shaped lines in populated areas. One procedure is to specify that the ratio of the population inside a district to the population inside a polygon just enclosing the whole district should be above a certain level. Unfortunately, a by-product of using such a measure is that it establishes a double standard of compactness for urban versus rural areas. Areas that are densely and uniformly populated face a more

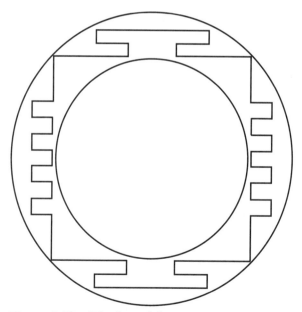

Figure 3.7b The jagged form passes.

stringent compactness requirement in effect than unevenly settled and less populated areas. Since groups that are protected under the Voting Rights Act tend to live in the urban areas, a criterion that restricts options to give fuller representation to their communities might well be challenged in court.

Conclusion

The technical aspects of redistricting are made necessary by the quantitative nature of the task and the immense volume of data that is needed to assess the racial and political effects of various proposals. However, the technical appearance of redistricting is somewhat deceptive. Redistricting choices are about more than mere numbers and shapes—they concern political power, fairness, and values of representation. Problems with reconciling these often conflicting values and choices are what we shall consider next.

CHAPTER 4

VALUES AND TRADE-OFFS

The quest for fairness and the pursuit of sectional advantage are as old as representative democracy. One frequently hears that the eventual goal of reforming the redistricting process is fairness, but what does that mean? At any point in time, people in the same state or country may disagree on the relative importance of various competing reapportionment goals, and over time what seems to be important about the process to one political generation may seem far less important to another. But above all, the problems involved in securing equitable solutions to reapportionment puzzles are complex because, at almost every point, principles or goals that everyone agrees to be desirable are in conflict with each other.

To illustrate, few would quarrel with these six propositions as valid goals for the redistricting process.

Considerations Involving Form

1. **Equal numbers** Congressional districts should be as equal in number as possible.
2. **Natural frontiers** Congressional districts should conform, where possible, to local boundaries, communities of interest, and lines of communication.
3. **Compactness and contiguity** Congressional districts should be as geographically compact as possible, and no part should be completely unconnected with the rest of the district.

Considerations Involving Outcome

4. **Party fairness** Congressional districts should be drawn to be as fair as possible between parties.

5. **Ethnic fairness**   Congressional districts should be drawn so that ethnic or other minorities have an equitable chance of representation.

6. **Party competition**   Congressional districts should foster party competition and alternation.

The first three considerations are in a sense technical or aesthetic, dealing with the ideal shape and size of constituencies in a fashion that is, ostensibly, politically neutral. But constituencies devised to meet these principles may not meet the political requirements of fairness to the various groups in the community, above all to the parties contending for power. In deciding a priority ordering for the six principles, most would start with equal numbers (although they might not have done so in the years before 1962), but after that, activists in the minority party might give higher priority to party fairness; ethnic and racial groups might select ethnic/racial fairness; city and county elected officials might opt for preserving communities of interest. As Miles' Law says, "Where you stand depends upon where you sit." According to certain ethical theories, values should be chosen for their intrinsic rightness, quite apart from their actual effects, but in the real world of politics, rightness and consequence are closely intertwined.

Without a consensus over goal priorities, it is impossible to agree how to resolve the inevitable conflicts between the values (Cain, 1984; Lowenstein and Steinberg, 1985; Grofman and Scarrow, 1982). Equal numbers may clash with ethnic fairness. Compactness may be at odds with the preservation of communities of interest. The philosophical case for each of these redistricting values and the potential conflicts between the six principles listed above will be examined more systematically in this chapter.

Redistricting Principles

One way to approach congressional redistricting is to devise a list of features that would be desirable in a district and to design seats so that these qualities are incorporated in them to the greatest extent possible. The principles listed above are the ones that are most commonly mentioned in thoughtful discourse on the subject. But what are the theoretical reasons for desiring these redistricting goals? In this discussion, we will treat these goals as ends in themselves—that is, as qualities of districts that might produce better or fairer representation. In Chapter 7, we will consider the procedural use of formal criteria (criteria 1–3 in our list) as a means of constraining the deliberate manipulation of boundary lines for partisan or racial advantage. There are, then, two ways of thinking about redistricting criteria. One is the intrinsic value they have for "good" representation. The other is the purpose they might serve to thwart deliberate gerrymandering. Our focus for the moment is on the first of these two values.

1. Equality of Numbers
It is technically possible, as we showed in the last chapter, to delineate constituencies that are almost exactly equal in numbers, but—as we shall see in a moment—there is a price to be paid. The problem is how much variation from this ideal should be tolerated in order to accommodate other important redistricting goals such as the preservation of established local government boundaries, compactness, or fairness to racial, ethnic, and political groups.

The chief characteristics of the American approach to population equality in redistricting are strict equality of numbers across districts and the use of total enumerated population as the basis for calculation. What is the justification for this from the standpoint of democratic theory? Clearly, the primary goal seems to be equality, but why? The usual rationale is that equipopulous districts give voters an equally weighted voice in the election of representatives. If one representative is elected in a district with ten times the number of constituents of another, then the influence of those in the larger district is formally ten times less than the influence of those in the smaller district.

This is bad for a democracy, one might argue, because it undermines the principle of popular sovereignty—that is, decisions with more popular support should be preferred over those with less popular support. While democratic societies might protect certain individual rights from tyrannical infringement by the majority, some form of majority or plurality rule is nonetheless the fundamental decision-making principle in a democracy. In order to arrive at an accurate calculation of the will of the majority or a plurality, each voice needs to be counted as equal. Malapportionment violates the principle of popular sovereignty by creating voices that are permanently unequal because of the skewing of district populations. By the same logic, reapportioning districts into equipopulous units reestablishes the conditions for popular sovereignty.

The scrupulousness with which a political system adheres to the doctrine of "one person, one vote" is related to the importance it assigns to political equality. Since the United States is strongly committed to the norm of individual political equity, it is not surprising that it has developed the strictest population deviation standards of any democracy using single-member constituencies.

But what justifies the second aspect of the American practice — equality of population rather than of voters? As we pointed out earlier, using general population rather than registered voters means that reapportionment produces districts with equal numbers of constituents, but not necessarily equal numbers of voters. The courts have rejected any attempt to move away from that tradition, drawing on the wording of the Constitution.

From the point of view of democratic theory, the key to a rational defense for the redistricting practice of using numbers of population rather than numbers of voters lies in the exact definition of voice. If voice is interpreted to mean voting only, then equality of population is an imprecise way of achieving popular sovereignty. However, if voice is taken to mean all the ways in which individuals might try to communicate with their representatives, and representation to mean representatives' activities on behalf of nonvoters as well as voters, then the justification for the current U.S. practice might be that it produces equal constituent voices in this broader sense. In fact, as we mentioned earlier, the practice of using the census lingers because of tradition and the Constitution, rather than deliberate philosophical choice. Our point is simply that, if one were forced to come up with a good reason for continuing this practice, the justification would rely on a doctrine of equal constituent representation rather than voter equity.

The goal of strict population equality, now a settled principle in the United States, may be at variance with the values of efficient representation and simple handling of constituency problems. To move electors from one district to another every ten years in order to make a decimal point difference in the ratio of electors to members can destroy established relationships without doing any good for anyone. Objectors in redistricting hearings sometimes complain about voters being switched from seat to seat in pursuit of mathematical exactitude; constituents and incumbents alike, it seems to some, are being crucified on a cross of statistics.

The strictness of the doctrine of population equality in this country is unique. The English boundary commissioners, charged with preserving natural boundaries, have allowed much larger deviations. At the last redistribution of seats in Britain in 1983, there was one seat of 95,000 and one of 48,000; a fifth of seats were more than 10 percent above or below the national quota. In Australia and New Zealand, 10 percent and 5 percent ceilings have been set on deviations from the average.

The case against frequent and exact redrawing of boundaries has gone by default. The abuses which led to the *Baker* v. *Carr* revolution still frighten people: Mathematically precise, up-to-date lines are a guarantee against rotten boroughs. Yet there are valid arguments for leaving boundaries alone as far as possible. First, allowing constituencies to incorporate natural communities of interest cannot easily be reconciled with the constant adjustment of district lines. Second, redrawing boundaries necessarily moves voters from one district to another, destroying any sense of contact they may have developed with their representative or with constituency-defined activities. Third, every redistricting necessarily opens the door anew to gerrymandering.

Moreover, even the United States allows for uneven representation when it comes to the least-populated states. This leads to the anomalous situation in which the within-state variations in congressional district populations are trivial, but the across-state variations are quite substantial. In 1980, the national average population for a congressional district was 519,000, but Alaska's one seat had only 400,000 while South Dakota's one seat contained 690,000. Nevada's two seats contained 391,000 and 395,000.

One other point should be made about equality of numbers. Representation is a two-way affair. There are the representatives as well as the represented. Equality in numbers for the latter does not mean equality in burden for the former. It may be much easier to move about a compact urban seat than a rural constituency stretching over hundreds of miles or crossing over high mountain ranges; this used to be one of the excuses for favoring rural over urban areas. On the other hand, a deprived inner-city seat may generate a host of special problems for its representative to solve. The mailbag of a member varies far more with the character of his or her seat than with the absolute numbers it contains.

2. Natural Frontiers and Communities of Interest

Respect for community boundaries and natural communities is a principle accorded much more priority by some states and countries than others. In Britain, where large numerical deviations are tolerated and where local government areas are more compact and uniform than in the United States, it is the most important concept guiding the boundary commissioners. In the United States, the diversity of local structures and the pursuit of exact equality of numbers lessens its importance as a guideline. But community themes are nonetheless echoed constantly in American redistricting.

Usually communities are defined in terms of local government boundaries—city and county borders—but these do not always coincide with other kinds of communities, such as ethnic and racial neighborhoods, topographical features, media markets, socioeconomic homogeneity, and the like. There is wide scope for argument about how a particular 'natural community' should be defined, and no one has yet offered clear answers to the general problem. There are places where ethnic groupings, occupational patterns, housing types, physical frontiers like hills and rivers, or simply local traditions do seem to identify a precise geographic area as a distinct community, but sometimes such lines are blurred or are not recognized by the inhabitants concerned. In such cases, any boundary must be arbitrary.

Furthermore, there seldom is complete agreement about which communities of interest are legitimate and which are not. To commercial developers, the zones of a new redevelopment project constitute a legitimate natural boundary, and they will lobby for city council lines that respect these zones. Ethnic neighborhoods and Catholic parishes are natural communities of interest to their inhabitants, but often not to the white middle class which tends to prefer traditional city and county lines.

What, we might ask, are the normative reasons for wanting to preserve the boundaries of local governmental units and communities of interest? Sometimes the case is made in terms of preserving tradition or the cognitive simplicity for voters in not having districts at various levels that crisscross one another. However, the more important reason stems from a particular theory of legislative representation that recognizes the importance of representing the interests of groups and communities as well as individuals.

The key elements of this underlying theory are that the representatives should be delegates, not trustees (at least to some significant degree), and that they should articulate the interests of important groups and communities in the district and not just the median preference of a disaggregated set of individual voters. To say that representatives must be delegates means that they have an obligation to give voice to all the interests and preferences of their constituents. This is in contrast with the viewpoint that the representative is elected to exercise his or her independent judgment. If the representative is meant to be a Burkean representative who is not obliged to focus on parochial district concerns, then seats do not need to be designed (and in fact should not be designed) to respect communities of interest of any kind. To do so would only place undue constituency pressures upon the representative. Thus, a communities of interest approach necessarily implies a delegate theory of representation.

The second part of the underlying theory behind a communities of interest approach concerns what the representative as delegate should represent. A purely individualistic approach maintains that members of Congress represent people, not deserts, beaches, industries, towns, or ethnic neighborhoods. The purest form of this position would make every district a microcosm of the whole state so that each representative was subjected to identical, unbiased pressures. If such an ideal could be obtained, representatives would represent the median preference of their districts, and the median of the legislators so elected would equal the median of the electorate at-large.

The alternative view is that representatives should represent the distinct interests of their districts, and districts should be designed to fairly reflect the continuum of interests in the electorate. If that reflection is sufficiently accurate, the outcome in the legislature could still be close to the median preference at-large, but it would be arrived at by aggregating diverse viewpoints in the legislature rather than identical viewpoints.

The second ideal requires more deliberate district design than the first. Purely random redistricting moves closer to the goal of individualistic representation, whereas careful crafting is required in order to secure a legislature truly reflective of the state's diversity. In recent years—especially in large, demographically varied states—the political reality is that the legislature must be diverse and reflective of major interests in the state or its legitimacy will be eroded. The communities of interest viewpoint has thus become more ascendant although, as we shall see shortly, it is limited by other considerations such as equipopulous districts, compactness, competitiveness, and the like.

3. Compactness

Compactness, as defined either by an area-based or a population-based measure, is most often discussed as a constraining criterion rather than as an intrinsic representational good. As we will discuss later, drawing oddly shaped districts is what most people mean by gerrymandering, and therefore a requirement of smooth, geometric shapes is regarded by some as the best method for preventing racial and political gerrymandering.

However, it is also possible to defend the principle of district compactness in terms of its intrinsic values. Two obvious considerations that come to mind are representational convenience and propinquity. The first holds that contorted and sprawling districts make it harder for representatives to do their jobs. If the districts cover too much territory, or if they cross rugged terrain with no natural access, parts of the districts may be cut off from the rest of the seat. Representatives may even feel deterred from visiting the remote sections of the seats as frequently as they should. Even when the geographical features of the districts are not a factor, a seat that zigs and zags through urban and suburban areas may have less of a sense of common identity than one that encompasses a compact area, making constituents more confused and ignorant than they would otherwise be about their representatives. Since there have been few empirical investigations of this subject, it is hard to tell whether any of the propositions are true. The argument for compactness based on representational convenience is closely connected to the previous case for observing communities of interest and natural boundaries. Hence, it is possible that if one observes the second criterion (i.e., communities of interest and natural boundaries) to the greatest degree possible, the argument for the third criterion (i.e., compactness) is usually moot; jagged lines may not matter if the districts' constituents all use the same media markets or if they share a common ethnic heritage. The strongest case for avoiding representational inconvenience probably arises when a district is both noncompact and violates the second criterion.

A somewhat different argument for compactness is based on the political interests created by geographical propinquity. Governments are in the business of providing public goods—services that have divisible costs and indivisible benefits. We can all be taxed separately to make contributions to paying for public goods, but many of these goods are provided to everyone, no matter what the size of their tax contribution. For example, when the police arrest the burglar who broke into your home, the seriousness of the investigation and prosecution should not depend on the size of your tax contribution. The voter's interest in these services is shared with others who live in the same geographic area; or to put it another way, the inability to exclude local public goods forges a common interest among people who live in a common geographic area.

Representation by geographic districts is a means for allowing common interests created by propinquity to be defended in the legislature. Many local public goods are provided by local and state governments, but many are at least subsidized by the federal government and hence are partially controlled by Congress. For instance, the placement or removal of a military base, the construction of a dam, and the dredging of a harbor are decisions that the federal government controls but which affect local interests because of propinquity. Thus, considerations stemming from propinquity can apply to congressional redistricting.

However, as with population equality, the critical question is "how much." If, as some would have it, the Court tries to establish a strict compactness standard (including perhaps a numerical guideline based on the formulas discussed in the previous chapter), will this significantly further the goal of representing the interests created by geographical propinquity? This is not something that can be determined in the abstract for all districts. Moreover, the case for compactness in terms of propinquity is also so similar to the one for the second criterion that, as with representational convenience, both the second and third criteria should be considered jointly. In other words, if compactness serves to represent a community of interest better (including one that hinges on propinquity and local public goods), then the case for strictly compact lines will be stronger.

4. Fairness between Parties

The first three criteria focus on the formal features of districts. But the way districts are constructed can also affect electoral outcomes. Criteria 4, 5, and 6 are standards that define what some consider to be desirable electoral outcomes, the prospects of which might be furthered by an enlightened redistricting.

The first of these concerns is the fair division of congressional seats between the major competing parties. At a minimum, partisan fairness in a democracy means that the party that receives a majority of votes should receive a majority of seats. This follows from the popular sovereignty principle. But often it is also seen to mean to people that the share of seats each party secures should match as closely as possible its share of votes, that is, that outcomes should be proportional to electoral support. While certainly not a requirement for a democracy, the principle of proportional representation seems to some to be a logical extension of the quest for greater political equity; that is, beyond the right to an equally weighted vote, some think it only fair that parties get seat shares that are equal to their vote shares.

However laudable the ideal, drawing boundaries for a single member, simple plurality system such as the one we have in the United States with a view toward achieving proportional outcomes is difficult for several reasons. Most importantly, under the first-past-the-post (i.e., simple plurality) system, party strength in the legislature is unlikely to reflect party strength in the electorate precisely. Between two major parties, a small majority in votes is likely to be exaggerated into a much larger majority in seats; minor parties never achieve anything like proportionate representation (except when they are tightly concentrated in a small subarea).[1] If all seats contained the same proportions of party support, then a party that won 50.5 percent of the vote would win every seat; but in that situation, it would need only a 1 percent nationwide swing to switch every seat to the other party. Reality, of course, is not like that; party support is never evenly distributed. Each side has pockets of great strength and total weakness, as well as some fifty–fifty situations. In every country that uses first-past-the-post voting there is a tendency for a disproportionate number of seats to cluster near the middle mark. A small movement in votes is always likely to transfer a disproportionate number of seats from one party to the other. In many situations a "Cube Law" seems to operate: If votes are divided in the ratio A:B, seats will split in the ratio A^3:B^3.[2] This explains how in Britain, Canada, and Australia so many elections produce landslide results even though the winning party's margin in votes is only a few percent. The only situation in which it could be guaranteed that the percentage of votes and the percent of seats would match exactly (i.e., A:B in votes produces A:B in seats) would be if the majorities in the various constituencies ranged evenly from 0 percent to 100 percent.

In the actual world, the distortions in the relation between seats and votes under the first-past-the-post system are not fixed, although they are often remarkably consistent. They depend on the prevalence of safe seats, and this will vary in different regions and at different times for demographic reasons; it will also vary with the extent of incumbent advantage—the ability of sitting members to defy national swings. The more the number of safe seats the more

---

[1] The Welsh Nationalist party with 0.4 percent of the U.K. vote has 0.5 percent of the 650 seats in the House of Commons. This is because it fights only the 38 seats in Wales and gets a substantial vote only in the five Welsh-speaking areas.

[2] See J. Curtice and M. Steed, "Proportionality and Exaggeration in the British Electoral System," *Electoral Studies*, Vol. 5, no. 3, December 1986, pp. 209–229.

proportional will be the relation between seats and votes. In the United States (and in Britain) the proportion of marginal seats (seats at risk to a 10 percent swing) has halved in the past thirty years. In 1958 there were 180 seats in Congress where the division of the two-party vote lay within a 60 percent and 40 percent range. By 1990 there were only 78 such seats. This trend was partly due to demographic changes—in particular to the movement of the affluent from the cities to the suburbs—but it seems more attributable to the increasing skill of incumbents in entrenching themselves—by personal publicity in the media and by frightening off potential challengers through the display of huge campaign chests. Therefore the electoral system produces results that are decidedly more proportional than they used to be. But no majoritarian single-member system will ever go all the way to proportionality. It is impossible to draw constituencies so that a nationwide or statewide swing of 1 percent in votes will produce a 1 percent swing in seats.

The long-term trend is even more spectacular, as Table 4.1 shows:

Table 4.1   Marginal Seats, 1874–1988

Year	Percentage of house where the two-party vote fell within the range of	
	35–45	45–55
1874	79.2	48.4
1914	63.7	29.6
1958	56.1	23.6
1988	32.9	7.4

SOURCE: D. Butler and S. Van Beek, "*Why Not Swing?*" PS (Summer 1990).

The growth in safe seats may make election outcomes more proportional in terms of seats and votes, but it may also gravely damage the interests of the group that has the most safe seats. Consider a city with ten seats in which Republicans constitute 41 percent of the electorate. Table 4.2 sets out three scenarios. If, at one extreme,

Table 4.2 Importance of Partisan Distribution Under District System

	Republican Seats, Percentage of Votes in Hypothetical Districts										Citywide (%)	Total Seats Won
Scenarios	(1)	(2)	(3)	(4)	(5)	(6)	(7)	(8)	(9)	(10)		
A	100	100	100	100	10	0	0	0	0	0	41	4
B	51	51	51	51	51	51	51	51	0	0	41	8
C	41	41	41	41	41	41	41	41	41	41	41	0

they were almost wholly concentrated in four seats (Scenario A), they would be certain of winning those seats but have no influence in the other six. But if they were evenly distributed among eight seats (Scenario B), each of these eight would be 51 percent Republican and would be won by them. At the other extreme, if they were evenly distributed throughout the city (Scenario C) they would have 41 percent in each seat and win none of them.

The real world rarely produces such simple examples, but every group devising boundaries in its own interest faces a challenge; it can either make sure of its representation by creating safe seats or it can gamble on having a larger number of winnable seats that are more marginal. Almost always the incumbents want to make their own seats even safer rather than sacrifice some of their party or ethnic support to a neighboring seat, even when this might offer a better chance of an additional gain for their side.

It is important to recognize that, even before the rules of strict redistricting equity developed as a result of *Baker* v. *Carr*, the electoral system worked with reasonable regularity and balance in determining party strength in Congress. Table 4.3 shows how, in every election since 1946, the party that won most votes won an even larger percentage of seats. On the only two occasions when the Democrats secured less than 50 percent of the House votes they lost their majority. On six of the eight occasions when they got more than 51 percent of the vote they got more than 60 percent of the seats. In only five out of the 25 elections did the percentage majority in seats fail to be at least twice the majority in votes. Whenever a party got over 54 percent of the vote, it secured a percentage of seats that was between 4 percent and 10 percent greater than its share of the vote. In short, while the system has not been made proportional by redistricting, it has normally satisfied the minimal conditions of popular sovereignty.

5. Ethnic Fairness
The United States, because of its tradition of widescale immigration and substantial ethnic and racial diversity, treats fairness to minority groups as an important redistricting issue. As with partisan fairness, there are two approaches, one minimal, one expansive. At

Table 4.3 Historical Congressional Seat and Vote Shares

Year	Democrat Share of Two-Party Votes (%)	Democrat Share of Seats (%)	Difference (%)
1946	45.3	43.3	−2.0
1948	53.0	60.6	7.6
1950	50.0	54.0	4.0
1952	49.9	49.1	−0.8
1954	52.6	53.3	0.7
1956	51.0	53.8	2.8
1958	56.0	64.9	8.9
1960	54.8	60.0	5.2
1962	52.5	59.4	6.9
1964	57.3	67.8	10.5
1966	51.3	57.0	5.7
1968	50.9	55.9	5.0
1970	54.3	58.6	4.3
1972	52.7	55.8	3.1
1974	58.3	66.9	8.6
1976	57.1	67.1	10.0
1978	54.4	63.7	9.3
1980	51.2	55.9	4.7
1982	56.0	61.8	5.8
1984	52.6	58.2	5.6
1986	55.0	59.3	4.3
1988	53.9	59.8	5.9
1990	53.4	61.4	8.0

a minimum, fairness means that significantly sized racial and ethnic minority groups are not excluded from representation in the political system. A stronger version of racial and ethnic fairness, like its partisan counterpart, is the principle of proportionality between population strength and legislative representation.

Both definitions of fairness are predicated on the assumption that minority groups are not geographically dispersed. As we mentioned before, any group, partisan or racial, that is too scattered cannot constitute a viable voting bloc in a single-member district system. Districts, for instance, cannot be drawn along sexual lines, because the populations of men and women tend to be intermingled almost equally. A district-based system can really only be fair to geographically concentrated groups. Thus, the treatment of political, racial, and ethnic groups in a district-based plurality system must be to some extent arbitrary. Interests that are optimally concentrated (i.e., neither concentrated too much nor too little) and of sufficient size tend to get more proportional representation. Blacks in many northern and western cities fit this definition. Nongeographical groups—women or left-handed people, for example—cannot hope to get representation by controlling the majority of voters in a district, although they might get elected with the support of nongroup members. Quasi-geographical interests are groups that are to some extent concentrated in one geographical area and can benefit from creative line-drawing. Latinos and Asians tend to fall into this latter category—they have distinct neighborhoods, but their population concentrations are not as great as the black community's and the shapes of their neighborhoods often do not have smooth contours. Much of the current dispute over racial and ethnic gerrymandering centers on quasi-geographical groups—on the extent of the state's obligation to avoid splitting a minority's support between different seats, or even further, to seek to unite minority neighborhoods into "minority seats."

The VRA and the courts have established that redistricting must take account of the interests of black and Hispanic communities under certain conditions. In the words of the VRA of 1965:

> No voting qualification or prerequisite to voting, or standard, practice, or procedure shall be imposed or applied by any State or political subdivision to deny or abridge the right of any citizen of the United States to vote on account of race or color.

As discussed earlier, the original VRA was amended in 1982 so that any institution or rule (including a redistricting) that had the effect of diluting minority strength, whatever the intent, could be proven to be a violation. If blacks or Latinos can show that they are sufficiently numerous in a given area to form a majority of a congressional seat, if they can demonstrate that they tend to act as a politically cohesive force, and if they can demonstrate a pattern of racially

polarized voting against them, then district lines that divide racial
and ethnic neighborhoods may be invalidated under the Act. In
other words, it is clear that the Act preserves racial and ethnic fairness in the minimal sense. What will interest observers more in the
1990s is whether the VRA will also be interpreted to cover fairness
in the sense of proportional strength. To date, both the Act itself and
the Court have explicitly said that there is no group right to proportional representation, but many critics believe that the Court has
already, *de facto*, moved close to that position (Thernstrom, 1987).

6. Competitiveness

Our last criterion is that elections should be competitive, and
therefore a significant number of districts should be inherently
marginal—that is, seats that could be won by the right candidate
from either side. The term used in political science is responsiveness. A responsive system is one in which small changes in the vote
result in relatively large changes in seat shares.

In the abstract, responsiveness is important to a democracy
because it provides a means for changes in preferences between
elections to be translated into changes in policy. If, for instance,
sentiment against further taxation increases over the period between
election 1 and election 2, then in a responsive system candidates and
parties who support greater taxation should suffer at the polls and
those who do not should do better. Changes in preferences would
ideally lead to changes in representatives and then to changes in
policy.

Unfortunately, in the real world, a number of things occur to
disrupt this scenario. The candidates who formerly supported higher
taxes might change their positions and get reelected (although this
still fits the basic ideal linking electoral and policy changes). Worse,
incumbent advantages in spending and resources might offset any
alteration in public sentiment about taxation, or incumbents might
find ways to obfuscate their true positions. But in principle, the
more electorally vulnerable incumbents are, the more likely it is
that, when public preferences shift, they will either change their
positions or be defeated.

But leaving the concerns of democratic theory aside, it is possible
to conceive of a two-party situation where all the seats are safe for

the incumbents, each getting 70 percent or more of the vote, so that even a massive nationwide swing of votes from one side to the other would make no difference to representation. It is also possible, even less realistically, to conceive of a situation where all the seats are in the 51–49 percent range so that a small swing would give them all to one side or all to the other. We discussed this logic of the electoral system on p. 76.

Many reformers consider that one of the goals of any redistricting should be to produce a dispersion of seats from safe to marginal that will make the legislature responsive, but not too responsive, to public opinion. It would be equally undesirable for an election where there is a clear but limited movement of support to produce no change in representation or to produce a 100 percent turnover. The problem, on which there is no agreement, is to decide what is the ideal degree of responsiveness to aim at.

But even if a goal were agreed upon, its achievement would not be easy. Seats do not continue indefinitely at a given level of marginality. Some become safer and some become more marginal. The figures in Table 4.3 showed how even within the past half century the relation between percentage of votes and percentage of seats has fluctuated. The variation has been limited but not negligible. Redistricting may affect the marginality of some seats, but the general competitiveness of the system is largely determined by long-term political forces such as the decline of party identification or the increasing resources of incumbents.

Conflicting Principles

We pointed out at the beginning of the chapter that almost all the generally accepted principles of redistricting can come into conflict with each other. Should equal-sized constituencies allow for residents who are not citizens and who are usually from an ethnic minority? Should equality of size be abandoned when that would help to produce party or ethnic balance or make constituencies more competitive? Should convenient local or natural boundaries be crossed or compactness be abandoned to ensure equal numbers? Figure 4.1 illustrates schematically these unavoidable conflicts of

Geographic considerations	National boundaries may not fit geographic units			
Compactness	Unwieldy districts versus equality	Natural features may run counter to compactness		
Party fairness	Weighting option excluded	Electorally punitive residential patterns	No necessary connection	
Ethnic fairness	Voters or total population	Ethnic population is dispersed	No necessary connection	Ethnic fairness may counter party fairness
Competitiveness	Weighting option excluded	Political homogeneity may create safe seats	No necessary connection	Proportionality creates safe seats	Ethnic fairness fosters non–competitive seats
	Equality of population	Geographic considerations	Compactness	Party fairness	Ethnic fairness

Figure 4.1 Matrix of redistricting values.

83

principle. A closer examination of the cells in this matrix reveals some of the complexity in a redistricting plan.

1. Equality of Population and Geographic Considerations
Representation of geographic interests was an important feature of early American representation. The U.S. Senate and many upper houses of state legislatures gave equal representation to unequally populated states and counties. The idea behind this kind of institutional feature was that less populated units and interests required protection from total domination by more populated units and interests. This kind of arrangement has survived in the U.S. Senate as a modern anomaly but has been eliminated at the state level. As a consequence, farming and rural areas generally have been less well represented since *Baker* v. *Carr*. To take another example, persons residing in coastal areas may have unique perspectives on oil drilling and environmental protection and may wish representational protection against more densely populated inland areas, but their needs must be accommodated within the framework of equally populated districts. The difficulty of handling this conflict has been graphically described by at least one distinguished jurist, Robert Bork:

> ... [G]iven the merciless requirement of a 1 percent deviation per district, the disparaties in population between census tracts, the inability to break the census tracts down further, and very uneven population concentrations across the state, the shape and size of electoral districts was determined by the corner of the state where we began to work. ... The rigors of arithmetic and inadequacies of the materials we had to work with meant that the new districts utterly ignored geographical and demographical facts. Small towns were split into two districts, people on opposite sides of rivers were lumped into single districts. There was no help for it, but editorial reaction around the State was often furious. One editorial was headed "Bork's Fiasco" (Bork, 1990).

2. Equality of Population and Compactness
Due to the low population density of rural areas and the relatively higher population density of urban and suburban areas, for rural districts to be equipopulous rural seats will have to be very large in

terms of square miles and urban districts much smaller. Moreover, if most of the population growth between decades occurs in the urban areas of a state, the rural districts will become more sprawling with each redistricting.

Most technical definitions of compactness, however, have little to do with the sprawling nature of districts *per se*, but rather with the contours and shapes of districts whatever their size. The need to create exactly equal populations may sometimes result in jagged edges, as tracts and blocks on the periphery are brought in to make district totals closer to equality. As a general rule, however, the equal population requirement does not cause dramatic violations of the compactness principle.

3. Equal Population and Party Fairness

When states have small variations in turnout among socioeconomically homogeneous populations, the equal population requirement by itself does not cause party unfairness. However, in states with large disadvantaged, nonwhite populations that tend to vote for the Democratic party, the use of census population data does have partisan implications. Because the census data includes a number of disadvantaged nonvoters, the Democratic party gets more representation than it would if voter data were used as the basis of reapportionment instead. In 1980, a conservative, Republican-leaning group argued in *Fair v. Klutznick* 447 U.S. 916 (1980) that the inclusion of noncitizens in the population data base used for congressional redistricting was unconstitutional. The Court dismissed the case on a motion for summary judgment, relying on the constitutional wording that refers to "counting the whole number of persons." For a similar reason, some residents of states that do not have large noncitizen populations feel that the apportionment process is unfair. Forty members of Congress from Pennsylvania, Kansas, West Virginia, Connecticut, Illinois, Michigan, Missouri, North Carolina, Oregon, Virginia, Wisconsin, Alabama, and Maryland took legal action in 1988 in a case called *Ridge v. Verity* Civ. Action No. 88-0351, alleging that the inclusion of the undocumented aliens resulted in extra seats for states such as California, Texas, and Florida, and fewer seats for states that contained small numbers of aliens. The case was dismissed in May 1989.

4. Equal Population and Ethnic Fairness

In addition to the Democratic party, disadvantaged minority groups also receive some advantage from the use of population data rather than registered voter data for redistricting purposes. The ratio of voters to population in Latino, Asian, and black neighborhoods is much less than in white, middle-class areas. As we saw earlier, redistricting with population data is a very inexact way to achieve 'one person, one vote," penalizing areas with high ratios of voters to population (i.e., high voting areas). Since the split between high and low voting areas also tends to run along racial and ethnic lines, the current practice benefits certain groups (e.g., blacks and Latinos) more than others (e.g., Italians and Irish). The Latino community, for instance, has a lower ratio of voters to population compared to other groups because their community has more noncitizens, more persons under 18, and more individuals with low educational backgrounds than average. Districting by voters rather than population would measurably diminish Latino representation.

5. Equal Population and Competitiveness

No serious conflict is involved. The fact that districts must be equally sized rules out various weighting schemes that might be devised to ensure that electoral outcomes are more proportional. For instance, if we knew that support for a given party was inefficiently distributed and that the party was unlikely to get its fair share of seats, one might in theory try to remedy the situation by making the districts controlled by the disadvantaged party smaller in population (just as rural districts before *Baker* v. *Carr* were smaller in size). This kind of remedial malapportionment, however, is clearly unconstitutional.

6. Compactness and Geographic Considerations

This is one of the most common choices that redistricters confront. The formal boundaries of local government units and the informal boundaries of communities of interest often take noncompact shapes. This is particularly true of newly expanded cities. In recent years, many cities, looking to increase their revenues from sales tax and to avoid additional burdens on their budgets, have annexed profitable industrial and commercial areas anywhere near their borders, leaving out other unprofitable nearby areas. Since compactness is rarely a consideration in annexation proceedings, districts that follow city lines will also be noncompact. In addition, of course, there is the irony that manipulation for gain at one level is treated sacredly by reformers at another.

7. *Party Fairness and Geographic Considerations*
The constraint of preserving formal or informal communities of interest can make it hard to achieve proportional party strength in a districting plan. When the electoral strength of a group is excessively dispersed by a districting plan, this is sometimes called "cracking," and when it is overconcentrated, it is sometimes called "packing." If for instance, a county is 95 percent Republican and that county is used to create most or all of the congressional seat, then the Republicans have been "packed" by the constraint of observing county boundaries. The reverse situation can also arise. If there is a pocket of Republicans in an otherwise majority Democratic city, then it may be "cracked" by a city boundary requirement.

8. *Ethnic Fairness and Geographic Considerations*
This is another extremely common choice in redistricting. Before the 1982 amendments to the VRA, there was no obligation to split city and county borders for the sake of ethnic and racial fairness. The only legal obligation was to avoid intentional discrimination. With the 1982 amendments, plaintiffs need only demonstrate that the plan has adverse effects to prove a violation. A districting plan that dilutes minority voting strength by refusing to cross city or county boundaries might well be in violation of the VRA.

9. *Competitiveness and Geographic Considerations*
One of the major obstacles to competitive districts is the socioeconomic homogeneity of residential patterns. In California, for instance, it is very hard to create a competitive district in largely conservative white, middle-class, suburban communities such as Orange County. The same is true of urban areas, with their large concen-

trations of nonwhite, disadvantaged populations. To the degree that these communities of interest are preserved by a districting plan, it will be harder to forge a number of competitive seats that could be won by either party.

10. Party Fairness and Compactness

A compactness requirement has no necessary or logical connection with electoral outcomes. As we will discuss in greater detail later, compactness can be used to constrain intentional partisan gerry-mandering, but outcomes can be unintentionally disproportionate regardless of shape. Depending upon the circumstance, a compactness requirement could lead to Democratic advantage, Republican advantage, or balanced outcomes. Some disagree. Lowenstein and Steinberg argue that compactness almost always leads to Republican advantage because it allows inner-city areas to be packed, but they fail to produce solid evidence on this point (Lowenstein and Steinberg, 1985).

11. Ethnic Fairness and Compactness

A compactness rule has little impact on certain inner-city minority groups. Because of the severe ghettoization of the black community, for instance, their neighborhoods and hence their districts tend to be compact anyway. This is less true of Latinos and Asians and of rural minority communities in the West and South. Area-based compactness measures inevitably restrict the freedom to draw noncompact districts for affirmative action purposes. Population-based compactness measures, as mentioned earlier, have the perverse property of requiring stricter compactness standards in urban than in rural areas and of placing yet another electoral burden on the nonwhite populations that live there.

12. Competitiveness and Compactness

Contrary to common wisdom, there is no necessary connection between drawing geometrically proportioned districts and the degree of competition in an electoral system. The competitiveness of a seat is controlled by many other forces, such as the power of incumbency and the political and social homogeneity of neighborhoods.

Square districts might or might not be more competitive than circular or jagged districts. Compactness can be used to make the process of drawing lines more neutral, but it does not guarantee fair outcomes.

13. Ethnic Fairness and Party Fairness

The creation of majority black and Latino seats can have the effect of diminishing the total number of Democratic districts. Before the VRA, minority neighborhoods could be divided up between various white Democratic seats to give each of them a solid base of loyal Democratic support. Unlike many white Democrats, black voters especially (and Mexican-Americans to a lesser degree) vote consistently for the Democratic candidate. "Cracking" minority neighborhoods into usable portions and attaching them to outlying white suburban seats might help white Democratic incumbents get re-elected, but at the expense of preventing minority communities from electing a representative of their own ethnicity or race.

14. Competitiveness and Party Fairness

As discussed earlier, the more responsive an electoral system, the less likely it is that it will yield proportional outcomes—a small change in votes can lead to a large shift in seats. A more proportional arrangement is not as responsive. This trade-off has led some to consider an alternative definition of fairness called symmetry, which guarantees only that parties get the same share of seats for any given share of the vote.

15. Competitiveness and Ethnic Fairness

Because inner-city black and Latino neighborhoods tend to be overwhelmingly Democratic in partisanship, "majority minority" seats are usually safely Democratic. Once a black or Latino is elected in a primary for such a district, the race is essentially over—more often than not, the candidate receives no or only token opposition in the November election. The only way these inner-city seats could be made competitive would be to join them with the outlying, usually suburban white neighborhoods, and this would probably not survive a challenge under the VRA.

Conclusion

Redistricting is at least implicitly about choices and trade-offs between competing principles and values. Certain criteria have primary importance because of Court rulings over the past twenty years. Districts must conform to the "one person, one vote" principle and cannot dilute minority voting strength. But after the primary criteria, there is a great deal of room for controversy over how trade-offs between the other competing values should be made. This makes the process inherently political in the broadest sense of the word.

CHAPTER 5

WHAT THE STATES HAVE DONE

Redistricting remains in considerable part an exercise in state action despite nearly three decades of decisions by the U.S. courts. The thrust of the successive Court rulings discussed in Chapter 2 has been to nationalize the importance of certain redistricting criteria—above all, "one person, one vote" and remedial fairness to racial/ethnic voting groups—and to outlaw certain state standards and traditional practices which would violate the so-called primary criteria. Nonetheless, the basic procedures and normal politics of redistricting are still protected by the principle of state sovereignty. States are free to decide such matters as whether to let legislators draw the lines as opposed to giving the task over to commissions, whether to use majority or supermajority voting rules on redistricting bills, and whether to mandate additional criteria beyond those required by the courts. The procedures they adopt influence the kind of redistricting politics likely to result.

A unique feature of the American system is that, while state legislators in all but eleven states draw their own lines, congressmen never do. This most sensitive task is, in all but three instances, delegated by one set of office holders (i.e., congressmen) to another (i.e., state legislators and governors). Apart from laying down the general principles for allotting seats to states, Congress has seldom interfered with the redistricting process. Bills that would have overturned, delayed, or modified the Court's rulings after 1962 were never able to muster the requisite vote in both the House and Senate. An effort to persuade the necessary number of states to go along with a constitutional amendment also failed. It consequently remains to the states, or failing that, the courts, to delineate congressional boundaries.

Congressmen do, of course, get involved in the process. Many are former state legislators with old friendships and alliances they can call upon. Others try to maintain close links with state and local officials so that they can have some influence over what happens to their seats. There have been instances, such as Virginia in 1981, in which the congressional delegation apparently distanced themselves from the process. Usually, however, the state's congressional delegation is allowed informally to submit proposals or make suggestions about what they would like to see. In an extreme case, California's 1981 redistricting, Congressman Phil Burton, a former state legislator and acknowledged redistricting specialist, was allowed complete autonomy in negotiating and devising the congressional lines. The Burton plan was never given a full public hearing and had no supporting documentation such as maps or basic statistics. Only a handful of state legislators were allowed to study the districts they were asked to vote upon. But this was an unusual case; ultimately, it is up to the state legislature to decide on congressional boundaries, subject to the governor's veto and the absence of objections from the state and federal courts.

As a consequence, the U.S. process is much more complex than that of other countries, which tend on the whole to have national commissions and uniform standards for all subsections of the country. In the pages that follow, we will examine state variations in redistricting procedures and political traditions. Apart from making plain the nature of this diversity, we will try to cast light on a group of central issues. Does institutional variation in the states relate to variation in redistricting politics? Why do some states tend to have more problems with partisan or racial questions than others? What has been the experience so far with attempts to reform the process by giving the task to commissions or the courts?

Variations and Similarities in State Procedures

On the whole, the procedures for congressional redistricting are more uniform than those for state legislative redistricting. For instance, only five states entrust congressional redistricting to commissions or neutral state agencies whereas four times as many states use a nonlegislative body for one or both of their house redistrictings. A common justification is that state legislators are perceived to have a distinct conflict of interest when they draw their own lines, but not when they draw congressional district lines. Another critical difference is that in seven states—North Dakota, South Dakota, Vermont, Wyoming, Alaska, Delaware, and Montana—there is no need for a congressional redistricting, because each has only one congressional seat. By comparison, in all cases but one (Nebraska), the states must redistrict both their lower and upper houses, which normally involves more districts and more complicated negotiations than in the congressional process.

The modal congressional redistricting procedure treats the redrawing of district boundaries like any other piece of legislation. In most states, there is no state constitutional deadline for completing the redistricting process. But Connecticut has set August 1991; Hawaii, 150 days after its commission is established; Indiana, April 30, 1991; Maine, 90 days into the 1993 session; Mississippi, 30 days before the first session after the census figures are available; Montana, 90 days after the census figures are available; Virginia, 1991 and Washington, 1992. Legislative leaders, including the chairs of the committees with jurisdiction over election law and reapportionment, fashion a plan after extensive consultation with some or all incumbent congressmen, interested legislative incumbents, and critical interest groups such as the Mexican-American Legal Defense Fund (MALDEF) or the NAACP, as well as local, city, and county officials.

This plan consists of "metes and bounds" (i.e., detailed street-by-street descriptions of district boundaries) or lists of the particular census tracts and blocks that are in each district. In addition, the legislature usually produces maps comparing the old and new lines and statistical descriptions of the new districts, including at a minimum their populations, the range of deviations from the ideal figure, and the percentages of nonwhite population. In addition, states that keep registration figures break them down by old and new districts. The legislators and congressmen, as part of the persuasion and negotiation process, also often receive much more extensive data on the outcome of past political races in their districts, which compare the party loyalty and ideological proclivities of lost and gained areas. These bills are then voted out of committee and onto the floor of the two houses of the state legislature, where they are debated, amended, and voted upon. The bill that passes in the legislature is then sent to the governor's office. The governor can sign or veto the bill. In the latter case, the legislature must usually get a two-thirds vote to override the veto. Table 5.1 outlines the procedures followed in the different states and clearly demonstrates the pervasiveness of this standard model.

The governor's veto is a varying threat. In North Carolina, there is no gubernatorial veto on any legislative matter, and in New York it cannot be applied to a redistricting plan. The supermajority vote needed to override the governor's veto is a critical barrier to a majority party's attempt to draw partisan lines. Except in one-party dominant areas such as the South, the majority party will normally lack the votes to override the veto. So if the minority party can gain control of the governor's office, it can force a better deal from the legislature or cause the matter to be resolved by the courts. This is why, for instance, the Republican National Committee and President Bush placed such a high priority on electing Senator Pete Wilson to succeed George Deukmejian in the 1990 California gubernatorial race. Having failed to gain control of the California legislature throughout the 1980s or to reform the process by initiative (including two competing measures, Propositions 118 and 119, on the June 1990 primary ballot), it was extremely important for the Republicans to hold the governor's office in order to prevent a repetition of what happened to them in 1981–82 when Democratic Governor Jerry Brown signed two sets of controversial redistricting bills designed by a Democrat-controlled legislature.

There are some slight variations in the form of the tool used to override the governor's veto. One state, Illinois, simply departs from the standard veto model by using a slightly different supermajority override rule—requiring three-fifths of the legislature instead of two-thirds. Three states—Idaho, Tennessee, and West Virginia—require only a simple majority to override the veto. This, in effect, renders the veto virtually meaningless as an obstacle to partisan redistricting since the dominant party in the legislature should be able to muster a majority vote with relative ease.

When a supermajority vote is required to override the veto, the governor's action can be critical to the outcome in split control states. In 1971 and 1973, California's Governor Reagan vetoed two separate redistricting bills sent to him by the Democrat-controlled legislature, because he and other members of the Republican party did not like the way that three of the five new congressional seats were drawn to favor Democratic candidates (California Redistricting, 1980). Another example was provided by the 1981 Colorado redistricting, in which Democratic Governor Richard Lamm rejected three congressional bills sent to him by the Republican-controlled legislature, because they would have given the Republicans a good chance at achieving a 4–2 division of the delegation. This forced the matter to the 3rd District Court, where the Democrats were rewarded with a plan that ultimately produced a 3–3 split (Cook, 1982, p. 1718).

On the other hand, governors have once or twice vetoed bills that were sent to them from a legislature dominated by their own party. This happened in Washington in 1981 when the Republican Governor John Spellman vetoed a congressional plan sent to him by a Republican-controlled legislature. Republican leaders had wanted to take advantage of their control over the process to create a new Republican seat by moving a Democratic-leaning city, Everett, out of a seat held by a Democratic incumbent, Al Swift, and into one held by a Republican, Joel Pritchard. This was opposed by all the Republican congressional incumbents, as one might expect, since incumbents tend to be risk-averse and are therefore more opposed than nonincumbent members of the party to the weakening of their districts for the sake of maximizing the size of the party's congressional delegation. Governor Spellman sided with the congressional incumbents and vetoed the plan, forcing the legislature to come back with a new bill that satisfied all the state's incumbent congressmen (Colford, 1982a, p. 1472). But usually, when one party has control of the executive and legislative branches of state government, governors sign the original redistricting bills that their legislatures forward to them. Thus when the 1990 California Democratic candidate for governor, Dianne Feinstein, promised that she would not rubber-stamp any redistricting bill sent to her by the Democrat-controlled legislature, her promise was not widely viewed as credible.

Table 5.1 Variations in State Procedures for Drawing Congressional Districts[a]

States	Seats in House of Rep.		Party Control in 1991			Initial Responsibility	Gov. Veto	Const. Article	Dead-line	Litig. 1980	Comments
	1982	1992	Gov.	Sen.	Assem.						
Alabama	7	7	R	D	D	Legislature	Y	N	N	N	Relatively neutral tradition
Alaska	1	1	Ind.	R	D	Single Seat	NA	N	N	N	Single Seat
Arizona	5	6	R	D	R	Legislature	Y	N	N	O	Turbulent politics make compromise difficult
Arkansas	4	4	D	D	D	Legislature	Y	N	N	O	Bipartisan plan in 1981 overturned by court
California	45	52	R	D	D	Legislature	Y	Y	N	U	Bitter debate 1981 led to several rounds
Colorado	6	6	D	R	R	Legislature	Y	Y	N	O	Gov. vetoed R plan in 1981. Court imposed neutral plan
Connecticut	6	6	Ind.	D	D	Back-up C	N	Y	Y	N	Stable situation since 1930
Delaware	1	1	R	D	R	Single Seat	NA	N	N	N	Single Seat
Florida	19	23	D	D	D	Legislature	Y	N	N	U	Relatively weak partisan tradition
Georgia	10	11	D	D	D	Legislature	Y	N	N	O	Democrats dominate reallocation
Hawaii	2	2	D	D	D	Comm. no Leg. role	N	Y	Y	O	Only slight adjustments made
Idaho	2	2	D	R	R	Leg. by 1993	Y	N	N	N	Stable since 1910

96

State										
Illinois	22	20	R	D	D	Comm. if Leg. fails by 8/91	Y	N	N	CP	Court overturned R plan and supported D scheme 1982
Indiana	10	10	D	R	D	Comm. if Leg. fails by 4/91	Y	N	Y	N	Bitter legal fights in 1982
Iowa	6	5	R	D	D	Comm. if Leg. fails, then Court	Y	N	N	N	At third attempt Leg. accepted revised neutral plan
Kansas	5	4	R	D	D	Legislature	Y	N	N	CP	First seat lost since 1961
Kentucky	7	6	D	D	D	Legislature	Y	Y	N	N	Stable since 1961
Louisiana	8	7	D	D	D	Legislature	Y	N	N	O	Stable since 1911, now loses one seat
Maine	2	2	R	D	D	Comm. but Leg. can overrule	Y	Y	Y	N	Stable since 1961
Maryland	8	8	D	D	D	Gov. but Leg. can overrule	Y	N	N	N	Numbers steady since 1961 but readjustment needed
Massachusetts	11	10	R	R	D	Legislature	Y	N	N	N	Gov.'s veto will be decisive
Michigan	18	16	R	R	D	Legislature	Y	N	N	CP	Compromise difficult over 2 seat loss
Minnesota	8	8	R	D	D	Legislature	Y	Y	N	CP	Stable since 1961
Mississippi	5	5	D	D	D	Legislature	Y	Y	Y	O	Stable since 1961 but readjustments needed
Missouri	9	9	R	D	D	Legislature	Y	Y	N	CP	1981 loss of 1 seat quietly compromised
Montana	2	1	R	D	D	Comm. no Leg. role	N	Y	Y	N	Single Seat

(cont'd)

Table 5.1 (*continued*)

States	Seats in House of Rep.		Party Control in 1991			Initial Responsibility	Gov. Veto	Const. Article	Dead-line	Litig. 1980	Comments
	1982	1992	Gov.	Sen.	Assem.						
Nebraska	3	3	D	Nonparty		Legislature	Y	N	N	N	Minor adjustments needed
Nevada	2	2	D	D	D	Legislature	NA	N	N	N	Bipartisan solution agreed with difficulty in 1981
New Hampshire	2	2	R	R	R	Legislature	Y	N	N	N	Stable since 1980
New Jersey	14	13	D	D	D	Legislature	Y	N	N	O	Court overturned D plan
New Mexico	3	3	D	D	D	Legislature	Y	N	N	N	Latino objection blocked conservative solution in 1981
New York	34	31	D	R	D	Leg. + Task Force	Y	N	N	U	Balanced compromise in 1981
North Carolina	11	12	R	D	D	Legislature	N	N	N	N	Divided Leg. foreshadows compromise
North Dakota	1	1	D	D	R	Single Seat	NA	N	N	N	Single Seat
Ohio	21	19	R	R	D	Legislature	Y	N	N	O	Split Leg. produced balanced cut in 1981
Oklahoma	6	6	D	D	D	Legislature	Y	N	N	N	Stable since 1951; R failed to block D plan in 1981
Oregon	5	5	D	D	D	Legislature	Y	N	N	N	Uncontentious plan for extra 1981 seat

Pennsylvania	23	21	D	R	D	D	Legislature	Y	N	N	U	R imposed plan in 1980
Rhode Island	2	2	D	D	D	D	Legislature	Y	Y	N	N	Stable since 1930; no problems
South Carolina	6	6	R	D	D	R	Legislature	Y	Y	N	CP	Stable since 1930; Court settled 1981 redistrict
South Dakota	1	1	R	R	R	R	Single Seat	NA	Y	N	N	Single Seat
Tennessee	9	9	D	D	D	D	Legislature	Y	N	N	N	Bipartisan agreement on new seat in 1981
Texas	27	30	D	D	D	D	Legislature	Y	N	N	U	Neutral tradition enforced by cross party voting
Utah	3	3	R	R	R	R	Legislature	Y	Y	N	N	Controversy over redrawing
Vermont	1	1	R	D	R	R	Legislature	NA	N	N	N	Single Seat
Virginia	10	11	D	D	D	D	Legislature	Y	Y	Y	N	D allocated first seat gain since 1950
Washington	8	9	D	D	D	D	2/3 vote Comm.	N	Y	Y	Y	1983 commission introduced after 1981 row over R solution
West Virginia	4	3	D	D	D	D	Legislature	Y[b]	Y	N	N	D Leg. has to divide 3 seats among 4 D congressmen
Wisconsin	9	9	R	D	R	D	Legislature	Y	N	N	CP	R Gov. blocked D plan in 1981
Wyoming	1	1	D	R	D	R	Single Seat	NA	Y	N	N	Single Seat

[a] Abbreviations: Gov, Governor; Litig., Litigation; Leg., Legislature; Comm., Commission; Ind., Independent; Y, Yes; N, No; NA, Not Applicable; O, Court overturned plan; U, Court upheld plan; CP, Court imposed its own plan. [b] Governor's veto can be overruled by a simple majority. SOURCE: Redistricting Provisions: 50 State Profiles. National Conference of State Legislatures, 1989.

After *Baker* v. *Carr*, a number of states sought to escape from the inevitable controversies by referring redistricting to a commission or some other neutral agency. In 1991 five states were committed to operate in this manner. Hawaii and Montana alone give their commissions both the original and the final right to decide district boundaries. In Connecticut, the task of reapportionment falls to a nine-member commission but only in the event that an eight member legislative redistricting committee, drawn evenly from both parties, fails to come to agreement. The five-man commission that will be in place for the first time in the state of Washington in 1991 must submit its lines to the legislature for a two-thirds vote before becoming law. Iowa gives the congressional redistricting responsibility to the nonpartisan Legislative Services Bureau, but final approval of its product is reserved to the legislature.

In the 1980s New Jersey offered a fascinating glimpse into the workings of a commission redistricting, albeit at the state legislative level. Because New Jersey holds its state legislative elections in odd years, it had to move exceptionally fast to produce new boundaries for use in 1981. It gave the redistricting task to a ten-person commission, five nominated by the majority leader and five by the minority leader. When this commission deadlocked, the state chief justice had to nominate a neutral eleventh member; he chose Professor Donald Stokes, a Princeton University political scientist. Stokes told the commission that he would draw up a strictly balanced plan; if they did not agree with it, he would invite each party to draw up its own plan and he would then vote for the plan closest to his. In fact, both parties produced virtually identical plans, but they still could not agree on the last details for a compromise between their differences, and so, on Professor Stokes' casting vote, the Democratic plan was chosen by 6 votes to 5. The Republicans subsequently complained that the chief justice had been partisan in selecting Professor Stokes, but according to Stokes, they had given tacit support to the outcome at that time. The whole process was completed in a mere two weeks of negotiation over alternative plans (Stokes, 1991).

In comparison to its state redistricting process, New Jersey has no such arrangement for settling congressional boundary disputes, and in the end, the matter has to be resolved by the Court. In 1981, the Democratic legislature drew up a proposal that was calculated to increase their party's share of the 13 congressional seats allocated to New Jersey. In one case, the plan pitted two Republican incumbents against each other and in another it pitted a popular Republican incumbent against a popular Democratic incumbent in a firmly Democratic district. This plan, which did increase Democratic representation by one in the 1982 election, was then overturned by the Supreme Court the following year in *Karcher v. Daggett* (1983). The Republican plan, which the Court imposed, was more faithful to the equal population rule by the narrowest of margins (a .69 percent difference). The Republicans won back one seat in the 1984 election because of the new boundaries and held it for the rest of the decade (Light, 1982b, p. 1190). In light of this, New Jersey has discussed a proposal to extend its commission procedure to congressional redistricting in 1991. If partisan issues are sufficiently contentious, it would appear from the New Jersey experience that no redistricting procedure is above criticism, although it does seem that the evenly balanced commission process produced something close to a bipartisan consensus.

It is interesting to note that no large state to date has shifted the congressional redistricting responsibility to a commission. The two most independent congressional redistricting commissions operate in states with few (i.e., Hawaii) or no seats to redistrict. In the other instances in which a commission or nonpartisan agency has the original jurisdiction over the task, the legislature has the final right of approval. The nature of this kind of relationship is well illustrated by the Iowa experience. In 1981 Iowa provided that its nonpartisan Legislative Services Bureau should draw up a congressional district map. The Bureau's actions were to be completely divorced from politics. Neither legislators nor outsiders were to be allowed access while this was being done, and the agency was mandated to follow strictly a political criteria—especially population equality and compactness. It was forbidden to use data such as party registration or even to make allowances for the home addresses of incumbents. If the legislature rejected a proposed plan, the Bureau was authorized to draw up a second and a third map. If these too were rejected, the legislature would then have to draw up a map themselves.

In the summer of 1981, the Bureau's first plan and then its second were rejected. Although they produced extraordinarily equal districts, they threatened two Republican incumbents, Tom Tauke and Jim Leach. While the process was neutral, the outcome certainly was not, at least in the eyes of Republican leaders. They regarded the plan as a Democratic gerrymander, and it was rejected by the state senate. Since the Bureau could not be publicly blamed for putting two incumbents in the same district (it was prohibited from taking such information into account by the legislature itself), the ostensible reason for rejecting the lines was that the population deviations (which were a mere 0.04 percent) were too large. Not surprisingly, the Bureau's second plan separated the two Republican incumbents, but it was still rejected because a Democratic leaning county was included in Tauke's district. That was removed in the third attempt, though yet a third Republican incumbent complained about getting the "hot potato" county. In the end, it seems that only growing public irritation against the protracted politicking led to legislative acceptance of the third plan (Duncan, 1982a).

When states become embroiled in partisan warfare over congressional redistricting, it can produce a great deal of bitterness and protracted controversy. As we noted earlier, partisanship was more of an issue in the 1981 round of redistrictings than it had been in the 1971 round. Partisan quarreling over new congressional boundaries usually centers upon two issues: incumbent displacement and partisan reconstruction of the districts. In regard to incumbent displacement, one of the parties, usually the minority party, may perceive that a plan unevenly distributes between the two parties the burden of losing former constituents or gaining new ones. Assuming that party strength is relatively equal in two areas, incumbents will generally prefer an area with constituents they have represented in the past to one with unfamiliar constituents. This is because incumbents typically invest a great deal of time, effort, and money in establishing name recognition and a favorable image. Years of mailing frequently into the district, of coverage by local newspapers, of countless visits to constituent meetings, and of innumerable acts of constituency service will have given incumbents a personal vote in the areas that they have represented. When familiar constituents are lost, the change represents a solid investment being thrown away and replaced by one that is risky and uncertain. Some displacement is obviously necessary to achieve population equality and to handle the "rippling" of changes in other parts of the state (Cain, 1984, Chapter 2). But there are usually degrees of freedom in this task and several ways to distribute the burden more or less equitably. When the incumbents of one party seem to bear a disproportionate share of the displacement burden, it will tend to incite partisan passions. To what extent has displacement been an issue in partisan redistricting battles? Table 5.2 lists the states that had partisan battles in the 1981 round of redistrictings and the issues that were at stake in each instance. From this, certain observations are possible. First, and most obviously, plans that place incumbents from the same party in the same district without their consent will cause partisan disagreement. Such a situation either forces one incumbent to run for a different seat or results in a costly primary fight, diverting money from critical November campaigns. At the same time, the placement of two minority party incumbents in the same district can solve problems for the majority party, especially when the state's total number of congressional seats is reduced; it can be advantageous to create open seats that the majority party would have a better chance of capturing if there was no incumbent.

The placement of incumbents from the same party in the same seat was an issue in four states—California, Illinois, New Jersey, and Pennsylvania. Pennsylvania provided an example of merging the seats of minority party incumbents in order to deal with a two-seat drop in the size of the state delegation (from 25 to 23). Four Democratic incumbents from urban areas in Philadelphia and Pittsburgh were combined into two seats. Democratic leaders accepted the need for some reduction, but objected to the fact that only Democratic incumbents were involved (Light, 1982a, p. 995). California offered a demonstration of this problem occurring even when the state was getting a greater share of congressional seats. The Burton plan combined the seats of six Republican incumbents into three seats in Los Angeles County. Burton formed the districts of Republican incumbents Bobbi Fiedler and Barry Goldwater, Jr. into one in order to open up a new San Fernando Valley seat for Howard Berman, a Democrat. In the process of rearranging areas in the eastern end of the county to create one new Latino seat (eventually won by Es-

Table 5.2 Partisan Redistricting Plans, 1982

State	Nature of Partisan Aggression	Aggressor
Arizona	Displacement of seat formerly held by Morris Udall to create a new safe Republican seat.	Republican legislature overrides Democratic governor veto with two-thirds vote
California	Displacement of numerous Republican incumbents, creation of four new Democratic seats, strengthening weak Democratic seats. Pairing of Goldwater–Fiedler and Rousselot–Moorhead.	Democratic legislature and governor
Illinois	Two Republican incumbents put in same district. Displacement of Erlenborn and Porter seats. Strengthening of weak Simon seat.	Court
Indiana	Displacement of Sharp, Evans, and Fithian.	Republican legislature and governor
Michigan	Displacement of Bailey (R) and Emerson (R) seats. Preservation of underpopulated Clay (D) seat.	Court
New Jersey	Collapse of Fenwick (R) seat. Strengthened Howard (D) seat. Two Republican incumbents in same district (Roukema and Courter).	Democratic legislature and governor
Oklahoma	Preservation of existing Democratic incumbents.	Democratic legislature and governor
Pennsylvania	Two pairs of Democratic incumbents in same district (Foglietta and Smith, Bailey and Murtha). Weakened marginal Democratic seat (Walgren).	Republican legislature and governor
Utah	Creation of new Republican-leaning district. Preservation of marginal Marriott (R) seat.	Republican legislature and governor
Washington	Creation of new Republican-leaning seat by displacing a Democrat.	Republican legislature and governor

SOURCE: Congressional Quarterly.

teban Torres) and to bolster the Latino population in a preexisting
district (eventually won by Marty Martinez), Burton placed Republican incumbents John Rousselot and Carlos Moorhead in one seat
and Wayne Grisham and David Dreier in another (Cain, 1985).
Even when all incumbents are kept in their districts, there are
other displacement issues that can become contentious. The minority party will often protest against redistricting changes that alter
their incumbents' districts beyond some baseline expectation. The
expectation that defines excessive change will often be based on the
initial population surplus or deficit (i.e., the amount that a district's
population differs from the ideal figure). If a minority party district
adds more new constituents or loses more former constituents than
is thought necessary to achieve population equality and if nothing
comparable happens to a majority party incumbent, this is likely to
be perceived as unfair.

This was the case in Arizona in 1981, when the Republicans
reconfigured the district of a Democratic incumbent, Morris Udall,
so that it comprised the Republican sections of Tucson and regions
with so-called disloyal "Pinto" Democrats (Light, 1982d, p. 161).
The drastic surgery performed on Bob Dornan's seat in California
to create a Democratic district for Mel Levine was another of the
many sources of contention in the Burton plan (Buchanan, 1982a,
p. 923). Similarly, in Utah, as well as in the Washington plan that
was vetoed by the governor, Democratic incumbents were forced to
absorb large new areas (Light, 1982e, p. 9).

The second major source of partisan contention, apart from displacement, is the partisan reconstruction of districts, the degree to
which redistricting trades make majority and minority party seats
weaker or stronger in underlying party strength. For instance, a
plan that systematically weakens the seats of marginal minority party
incumbents or strengthens the seats of majority party incumbents
makes it more likely that a seat will change hands from the minority
to the majority party. Once again, the Burton plan provides a good
example because it strengthened the Democratic registration in the
marginal George Brown and John Burton districts and weakened
the Republican registration in the Clausen and Dornan seats (Cain,
1985). In the less successful Indiana Republican gerrymander, the

thrust of the plan was to concentrate Democratic strength to the greatest degree possible in three or four districts and to spread Republican strength more evenly in order to capture the remaining six or seven districts (Buchanan, 1981).

Although this process is quite clearly apparent in specific instances, is there any evidence that, under conditions of single party control, the majority party support tends to even out (i.e., make more efficient) the pattern of support in majority party seats and concentrate (i.e., make more inefficient) the support in minority party districts? One way to test this is to find a common measure of party support and to see whether, in states where one party has control of redistricting, there is any relation between previous levels of partisan strength in individual districts and possible weakening or strengthening by the trades involved in redistricting.

While registration figures are lacking in many states, it is possible to use the Democratic vote in the last presidential election in both the pre- and postredistricting seats. If seats that were already strongly Democratic were made less so and those that were marginal were made more Democratic by this measure, then there should be an inverse correlation between the Democratic vote in a district before and after redistricting when the Democrats controlled the process. The same logic applies for the Republicans when they controlled the process. In fact, that is what we find, although the correlations are fairly modest. In the Democrat-controlled states in 1981, the bivariate Pearson correlation is $-.38$ and significant at $p < .01$, and in the Republican controlled states, it is $-.58$ and also significant at $p < .05$ (Cain and Campagna, 1987). Thus, the pattern is not something that chance would have produced. It is important to remember, of course, that this may or may not have the desired electoral impact, as the widely divergent outcomes in California and Indiana show.

An alternative approach is to look at the plans agreed upon without partisan controversy. Two common elements can be found in the experiences of states with bipartisan redistrictings in 1981. First, the plans are less likely to be controversial when they make no significant changes to existing boundaries. Connecticut has provided a good example of this. Since the state's population had changed very slightly, it was not necessary to make major alterations in the district boundaries of either party's incumbents. Attempts to instigate partisan mischief were successfully beaten back. Republicans proposed to make changes that would weaken the marginal seats of two Democratic incumbents, William Ratchford and Toby Moffet, but when the legislative panel deadlocked, the commission opted for less controversial proposals that seemed to preserve Democratic control of both seats (Colford, 1982c, p. 129).

The other characteristic of bipartisan plans is that when drastic changes have to be made, political burdens are doled out in a more even-handed fashion. For the fourth decade in a row, New York had to reduce the size of its congressional delegation (by five seats in 1981). Moreover, the inner-city Democratic areas of the state exhibited the lowest rates of population growth. In a partisan plan, Democrats would have absorbed a greater share of the seat collapses and displacement. In their bipartisan plan, the legislature combined incumbents in a manner that would cost each party two seats (i.e., pitting two pairs of incumbents from each party against one another), and then set up a "fair fight" in the fifth, pitting a Democratic incumbent, Peter Peyser, against a Republican incumbent, Benjamin Gilman (Light, 1982c, p. 1913). In short, New York produced a bipartisan plan by splitting the differences between the parties and sharing equally the burdens of adjustment.

Conditions Leading to Partisan Disputes

Granted that bipartisan outcomes are more common than partisan ones, can we say anything about when the latter are more likely to occur? Research points to one key factor, single-party control of the state legislature and of the governorship (Erikson, 1972). However, single-party control was not a sufficient predictor of partisan redistricting in the 1980s. In Alabama, Florida, Iowa, Maryland, Massachusetts, Mississippi, North Carolina, Rhode Island, and West Virginia, the legislature and the governorship were controlled by the same party, but no partisan battle ensued.

Why do partisan disputes occur in some states but not others? The explanation must have two components: the political considerations that induce a majority party to try to gain extra seats during redistricting and the institutional arrangements that make such an attempt successful. In the case of state legislative as opposed to congressional redistricting, it is easy to see that party caucuses in the state legislature would prefer to increase their shares of seats. The majority party wants to retain control of the legislature, and the minority party will want to become the majority. The more balanced partisan strength in the legislature is, the more likely it is that the redistricting process will be partisan, since the gain or loss of a seat might affect which party controls the legislature.

By the same logic, once one party has safe control of the state legislature, the incentive to add to its delegation by means of redistricting should decrease. To put it another way, after a majority party has achieved a certain winning size, it should find diminished value in adding more members to its caucus. At a certain point, it is even conceivable that a majority party might become worse off by adding new members, for instance, because there would not be enough committee and subcommittee chairmanships to go around, or because the ideological heterogeneity of the party legislative caucus would increase to an unmanageable level.

Congressional lines, however, are not drawn by members of Congress, and one may ask how partisan considerations in the legislature spill into the drawing of congressional seats. Of course, there may be self-interested considerations: State legislators may want to enlarge their party's congressional delegation so that they will have more potentially winnable (or at least open) seats to run in the next election. State legislators are also likely, of course, to have closer ideological and personal ties to the members of their own party's congressional caucus than to those of the other party. Additionally, general party competitiveness in the state may affect the willingness of legislators from different parties to cooperate with one another. Residual bitterness over policy or budgeting issues can make state legislators less likely to agree on congressional redistricting bills as well as over other matters.

As we have suggested already, if a state has gained or lost congressional districts in the apportionment process, redistricting will necessitate difficult decisions over which the parties may disagree. On the other hand, if national apportionment dictates that the size of a state's delegation remain unaltered, any boundary revision will probably be less significant and hence less likely to cause partisan tensions.

Whatever the political conditions, a majority party cannot obtain what it wants unless certain institutional arrangements are present. One critical factor is single-party control, defined as control by one party of both houses of the state legislature and of the governor's office. Divided control, as we have seen, will serve to check the majority party.

But another contributing institutional factor is the voting rule employed by the legislature. The smaller the coalition needed to win, the easier it will be to put together a majority winning coalition and the more likely that this will occur. If the legislature employs a majority rule, then the majority needs only to hold its members together in order to pass a bill through the legislature. If a two-thirds or other supermajority rule is required, then the majority must either be large enough to comprise the necessary two-thirds or be able to win over some minority party votes.

In sum, a partisan dispute is more likely when the parties in the legislature are more competitive, when one party controls the process, when the legislature's voting rule in deciding the redistricting bill is a simple plurality or majority, and when demographic changes dictate the addition or subtraction of at least one seat from the state delegation.

It is possible to test the explanatory power of these factors (Cain and Campagna, 1987). Let us set up a simple model that predicts the odds of a partisan plan as a function of

1. Whether a state redistricting process is controlled by one party (coded 1 = yes).
2. Whether a state uses a majority or supermajority rule (coded 1 = majority rule).
3. A measure of state competitiveness (1 divided by the percentage of legislative seats held by the majority party in 1980).
4. The apportionment status of the state (coded 1 if there were no changes in the number of congressional seats a state got through apportionment).

The first three conditions must all be in force in order for a partisan redistricting to occur. A majority might have single party control but might not be able to implement its plan if it needs a supermajority vote. Or it might have the institutional conditions but not have the political incentive because one party is so dominant. The estimated logit coefficients are as follows on the basis of what happened in the 1981–82 redistricting:

Prob (Y = Partisan dispute) = [4.55(.29) − 1.04(.45) No change in state delegation size + 61(.29) single party control × competitiveness × majority vote rule] χ^2 45.

In other words, the model tells us that no change in a state's delegation decreases the likelihood of partisan controversy, *ceteris paribus*. The interaction of all three conditions also significantly increases the odds of a partisan redistricting agreement. For example, a state like California would be expected to have redistricting troubles in 1981 because its political competition was intense, it had single-party control of the process, it used a majority rule in the legislature, and it had to add two seats to its delegation. Mississippi had a number of these conditions but was not politically competitive.

Courts and the States

So far, we have focused on the outcomes of legislative redistrictings of congressional seats, but in twenty-three states the courts had the final say in a state's reapportionment. Court involvement in the past has had several different forms. In seven states in 1981—Michigan, Minnesota, Missouri, Colorado, Kansas, Illinois, and South Carolina—the district courts had to take over the line-drawing because of a political impasse at the state level. In all but one of these cases, the state government was divided between two parties, and the governors' vetoes forced matters into the courts' hands. In Michigan, Illinois, Missouri, and Minnesota, Republican governors vetoed the plans of Democratic legislatures, and in Kansas and Colorado, the party positions were reversed. South Carolina, the one exception to the relationship between split government and court intervention, became stalemated because rival Democratic factions in the two houses of the state's legislature could not agree about how to make relatively minor changes to the state's six congressional districts. In the end, the district court drew a map that was very close to one of the proposals that emanated from the lower house, much to the dismay of the state senate faction. What is remarkable about the six divided government cases is that in all instances the Democrats seem to have obtained more of what they wanted from the courts' plans than the Republicans have. In Michigan, the Republicans could point to the fact that two of the three judges on the federal panel that selected the Democratic legislature's plan over the Republican proposal were themselves Democratic appointees. (The plan at least conformed to familiar political logic.) But in Illinois, the three-judge panel had a 2–1 majority of Republican appointees and still chose a plan devised by the House Democratic leader, Michael Madigan, and his hired consultant, Kimball Brace.

The courts might perhaps be expected to side with the legislature because redistricting has historically been the legislature's prerogative. Since the Michigan and Illinois legislatures were controlled by the Democrats, the courts were simply reacting to what was on the table. This is plausible, but it does not explain why the Democrats also did better than the Republicans in the courts' plans for Kansas and Colorado. After Kansas's Democratic governor, John Carlin, vetoed two redistricting bills passed by the Republican-dominated legislature, the court selected a plan proposed by a Democrat, state senator Jack Steineger, which placed a liberal stronghold (Douglas County) in a marginal Republican seat belonging to incumbent Jim Jeffries. Jeffries announced his retirement shortly thereafter rather than fight the opposition in the new seat (Colford, 1982b, p. 1724). As discussed earlier, Colorado Republicans had hoped to gain a majority of the state's six allotted congressional seats, but after the Democratic Governor Lamm vetoed three plans devised by the Republican legislature, the court opted for a plan that retained the incumbents and preserved the partisan balance of the delegation.

A better observation might be that in most instances the courts seem to select plans that rock the boat the least while at the same time rigorously adhering to "one person, one vote" requirements. Thus, in Michigan, Colorado, Kansas, South Carolina, and Missouri, the courts' plans tended to preserve all incumbents and re-sisted the temptation to rearrange the political landscape *tabula rasa*. But here too there are counterexamples. The Illinois plan collapsed four Republican seats into two and reconfigured the state signifi-cantly in an effort to preserve three predominantly black Chicago districts (Benenson, 1989, pp. 2980–81). The courts' greatest de-parture from drawing lines to preserve the status quo came in Min-nesota when it abandoned the traditional even division of the state's eight districts between rural and urban areas and gave a 5–3 edge to urban areas, displacing every incumbent and placing four con-gressmen (three Republicans and one Democrat) into two seats (Buchanan, 1982b, p. 2000). Thus it would appear that there may be no simple lessons to be inferred from the courts' 1981 forays into line-drawing other than the obvious one—namely that if a court adopts a plan that is proposed by or seems to benefit someone from one party, the odds are that it will displease a number of people in the other party.

However, in a majority of cases the courts are asked to review the constitutionality of the district lines drawn by the legislature rather than draw district lines themselves. The reason for this is simple. In general, legislators will prefer to make the necessary compromises in a divided government situation with members of opposing par-ties in order to retain the opportunity of drawing their own lines: The certainty of something less than an incumbent's ideal district is usually better than the uncertainty of a court drawn plan. As we have seen, the courts' behavior when they have the responsibility of creating a new plan is unpredictable. They might pick the major-ity party's proposal, they might adopt the minority party's proposal but amend it in critical ways, or they might start from scratch and completely upset the pattern of traditional district lines altogether. However, taking the experience of the 1980s as a guide, it would appear that in keeping with their general caution about this po-tentially intensely political exercise, the courts will usually attempt to preserve the *status quo* to the greatest degree possible given the changes needed to make equally populated districts.

If this holds true in the future, the party with the most to gain by throwing the redistricting process into the courts is that one that benefits by keeping things as they are. In 1981, Congress had a large Democratic majority, and yet the Republicans had won control of the presidency and the Senate. Many Republican office-holders and some political analysts believed that realignment was around the corner, especially since the districts with the greatest population deficits were more often in inner-city, Democratic areas of Los Angeles, Detroit, New York, and St. Louis than in the surrounding middle class, more Republican suburbs. Republicans naturally wanted districting changes that accurately reflected the trends in the underlying demographic and political currents. Democrats simply wanted to hold on to what they had. In 1981 at least, the federal courts' conservative, *status quo* instincts consequently better matched Democratic rather than Republican party interests.

In their more common role as reviewer rather than author of districting plans, the courts overturned 11 plans and upheld five. The courts inspected three kinds of cases. The most frequent involved black and Latino districts. In Georgia, Louisiana, and Mississippi the courts overturned parts of the legislatures' redistricting plans in order to strengthen the electoral power and representation of black constituents. The Georgia case offers a good illustration. Although the state had grown by nearly one million during the 1970s, it did not qualify for an additional seat. African-American leaders tried to persuade the legislature to make a majority black district out of one incumbent's seat. They managed to get the state senate to pass a plan that created a 69 percent black district based in Atlanta, but the Georgia house reapportionment committee rejected this option because it placed two white incumbent congressmen into one district. The legislature's plan was overturned by a federal court, which determined that blacks were entitled to a district that was at least 65 percent black. A white incumbent, Wyche Fowler, continued to hold the reconstructed 5th Congressional District until 1986 when he ran for the U.S. Senate. The district finally elected a black representative when John Lewis defeated Julian Bond for the open seat (Menendez, 1981, p. 2403). In a similar fashion, the courts ordered the redrawing of Louisiana's heavily black 2nd Congressional District in New Orleans and of Mississippi's 2nd Delta Congressional District.

Latinos also won some victories through court action. In Texas, for instance, African-Americans and Latinos filed suit in objection to the legislature's districts in south Texas, the Dallas–Fort Worth area, and Houston. The districts were first reviewed by the Justice Department, which objected to the packing of Latinos in the 15th Congressional District (an 80 percent Latino seat) and the dilution of Latinos in the 27th (52 percent Latino). When the Republican Governor Clements refused to call the legislature into special session to redraw those seats, a federal three-judge panel adjusted the two districts to even their Latino populations (Duncan, 1982, p. 1752). Minority plaintiffs do not always prevail in these actions. For instance, the court upheld the Pennsylvania congressional redistricting plan when minority plaintiffs filed suit charging that district lines in a Pittsburgh area seat diluted minority voting strength. It is important to remember, however, that these cases were decided before the Supreme Court's decision in *Thornburg* v. *Gingles*, and the standards for proving a violation are clearer now than they were in 1981. A number of states and cities are covered by Section 5 of the Voting Rights Act, and in those places, the courts wait for the Justice Department to review district changes before they act. But the revamped language of Section 2 provides an important path that will lead to a great deal of more racial vote dilution litigation in the future.

A second sort of constitutional review performed by the courts in 1981 involved population cases. Arkansas' districts were overturned for having a 2 percent population variation. As discussed earlier, New Jersey's congressional districts were also overturned for having excessive population deviations, but it is likely that the Supreme Court was really using the population issue in this case to signal its discontent with the partisanship of the districting plan. In Hawaii, the population deviation problem arose because the state used registration data instead of the Census Bureau's total population figures. The Court struck down the state's congressional plan, because the use of registered voter data led to a 3 percent population deviation as measured by the census data. Hawaii, it ruled, could only use an alternative data set if it would result in the equivalent of a plan that used total civilian population.

The third and least frequent form of review in the 1980s involved partisan gerrymandering. These included the Democratic challenge to Indiana's state legislative districts in *Davis* v. *Bandemer* and the Republican challenge to California's congressional plan in *Badham* v. *Eu*. As compared to the racial vote dilution challenges, plaintiffs have not yet been successful in these cases, although they may have achieved a significant victory by getting the Supreme Court to rule that partisan gerrymandering is justiciable. To date, then, this has been the least common form of court intervention.

As this review of court actions in the 1980s clearly shows, the courts have been drawn into the political thicket of redistricting in a variety of ways. The most conventional form of involvement, reviewing the constitutionality of redistricting plans passed by state legislatures, has been expanded by the broadened definition of vote dilution and the evolving strictness of its equal population standards. Moreover, with the decline of partisan loyalties in the United States generally and the rising number of divided state governments, the courts have increasingly been asked to decide between competing plans or to devise districts from scratch. Unless more states adopt backup commissions with tie-breaking mechanisms, the prognosis for the following decades must be that the courts will find themselves in the uncomfortable position of drawing congressional lines more frequently in the future.

Conclusion

Redistricting remains an exercise in federalism, but variations at the state level in procedures and standards could be substantially diminished in the future. The doctrine of "one person, one vote" has eliminated certain long-standing state practices, such as basing state senate seats on counties (i.e., the federal model) and strictly adhering to county lines as the basic building blocks for congressional and state districts. But the redistrictings of the last two decades have amply demonstrated that "one person, one vote" still leaves a lot of room for political machinations. The 1982 amendments to the Voting Rights Act together with the so-called Gingles criteria (discussed in Chapter 4) decree that, where it is possible, African-American and Latino seats should be constructed to be as close to 65 percent minority in composition as possible. The courts arrived at this standard in a more or less ad hoc way. They assumed that a minority group could only control its electoral fate if it had a majority share of a district's population, but then they allowed an additional 5 percent for various disadvantages African-Americans and Latinos typically suffer (e.g., being poor, having a larger share of underage constituents). In this way, the courts' explicit definition of a constitutionally protected minority seat has created a particular kind of uniformity in redistricting practices across the states in these districts.

But there remains a great deal of latitude in how most seats are constructed, since the Voting Rights Act does not apply to them. However, if the Court decides to develop a more explicit definition of vote dilution and to take a more aggressive position toward political gerrymandering, this could introduce yet more uniformity in state standards.

Finally, a third potential source of standardization is political. If the political process becomes increasingly stalemated by split government, and if groups come to believe that the courts' criteria and approaches will be more advantageous to them than the political process (a belief more likely to be held by party activists and leaders than incumbents), then the courts may find that they acquire the role of redistricter more often. Since the courts tend to stick extremely closely to their own criteria, this would likely further dampen state variations.

CHAPTER 6

WHAT THE REST OF
THE WORLD DOES

The American approach to redistricting is quite different from that of most other democracies. The task of drawing new boundaries in the United States still resides primarily in legislative hands whereas this is no longer true in many other democracies. Also, most Americans accept the fact that redistricting has been and will continue to be a politically sensitive matter. But in some countries, redistricting has been relatively uncontroversial. In 1987, Australia redrew its 125 constituencies into 148; no boundary was left unchanged, but in a very political country there was hardly a murmur of complaint. In India and New Zealand, redistricting has been carried on with very little stir. The arguments in Britain and Canada have earned a few headlines, but the acceptance of commission-devised proposals has been relatively placid. Only France among the major democracies with single-member constituencies has left redistricting to the government of the day—and even there controversy has been dampened down by the existence of legal remedies.

To make this point is not to suggest that the United States is missing out on some simple formula that would solve the complex problems that confront state legislatures and courts every ten years. The neutral commission, which almost all other countries have used, has been tried in the United States. It has had very limited success. The American political tradition sets it apart from other democracies. Attempts to remove redistricting from the pressures of incumbents and interest groups would likely be undermined by other features of the American system.

117

Americans seldom realize how exceptional their version of democratic government is. The United States is not alone in electing its legislatures from single-member districts. But when it comes to the problem of how to draw up such districts, American practice has diverged more and more from those employed elsewhere. During the nineteenth century in Europe and the self-governing colonies around the world the drawing of boundaries was left to the legislature almost everywhere. Deals between government and opposition and pressures from individual members played a very large part in amending any bureaucratic suggestions for new boundaries. Gerrymandering and tough politics were as much a part of the British and Australian arrangements as they were in the United States. But in the last few generations the idea that party politicians are best excluded from anything so central to their fate has developed. In all the Commonwealth countries the legislators have more or less opted out, leaving the process to neutral commissions.

In the United Kingdom the idea that constituencies should have roughly equal electorates was only accepted in 1918. But following the redistribution of that year, boundaries were left alone for a generation and wild divergences in numbers developed; by 1939 constituency electorates varied from 15,000 to 150,000. It was only in 1944 that permanent boundary commissions were set up in the United Kingdom, charged with producing comprehensive proposals for the redistribution of parliamentary constituencies every three to seven years. What follows will refer to the Boundary Commission for England, although the separate bodies for Scotland, Wales, and Northern Ireland operate in virtually identical fashion. Since 1958 the routine interval has been extended to every ten to fifteen years. Thus, following new boundaries in 1950 and 1955 there were fresh proposals in 1969 (given effect in 1974) and in 1982 (given effect in 1983).

The Boundary Commission, although nominally chaired by the Speaker of the House of Commons, is effectively run by its vice-chairman, a High Court judge. It has two other members (usually lawyers) and two assessors (the director general of the ordinance survey and the registrar general). It has a civil service staff of ten or so, jointly headed by one official from the Census and one from the Home Office.

Boundary commissions were used in the nineteenth century, but their findings were sometimes altered by party deals in Parliament.

In this century Parliament, with two exceptions, has never significantly revised the proposals prepared by neutral boundary commissioners. The two exceptions were not concerned with specific constituencies. In 1948 a Labour government, believing that urban areas were underrepresented, asked the commissioners to devise seventeen extra seats. There were cries of foul from the Conservatives, but actually the seats divided almost evenly in the next election. It should also be noted that the general effects of this comprehensive redistribution cost the Labour Party, which carried it out, about 30 seats—enough to deny the party power for much of the 1950s.

In 1969 the next Labour government, worried about the seats it would lose under a general redistribution, postponed implementing the Boundary Commission's proposals on the ground that an impending change of local government boundaries would render them obsolete. Once again there were shrill protests from the opposition—and ministerial diaries now reveal how consciously partisan were the motives behind the delay.

The English Boundary Commission operates under strict but confusing statutory rules. It is required to respect local boundaries "as far as possible" and it is required to make constituencies "as equal as possible." These two principles repeatedly conflict, and the commissioners have never had a consistent policy in deciding between them. In 1982 the Labour Party brought suit, unsuccessfully, against the Commission for giving too much weight to "natural communities" and too little weight to equal numbers (Waller, 1983).

The Commission establishes an England-wide quota for electorates by dividing the latest annual register of the electorate by the current number of seats. For the 1983 redistribution, the quota was 65,700. The Commission then allocates the appropriate number of seats to each shire county (ranging from 4 to 15) and to each metropolitan county (ranging from 13 in Tyne and Wear to 84 in Greater London). It accepts county boundaries as inviolable and its initial allocation of seats as virtually unchangeable.[1] It then

---

[1] But the way in which the commissions have dealt with surpluses in the quota and their occasional uses of their discretion to create an extra seat has led to a steady growth in the size of the House of Commons: 1950: 625, 1955: 630, 1974: 635, 1983: 650.

draws up a provisional map which is published for objections to be raised.

If there are objections, local inquiries are held by assistant commissioners (who are working barristers, appointed *ad hoc* for the job). They listen in public hearings to the views of local councils, local political parties, and private citizens, and they then report to the boundary commissioners in London who usually, but not always, accept their recommendations. The reports and the reasons for accepting or rejecting them are made public. If the commissioners vary their original proposals, there is the possibility of holding a further inquiry.

Neither the commissioners nor the assistant commissioners are supposed to have any cognizance of political party consideration. Compactness, established geographic links, natural and administrative boundaries, and communities of interest are the only relevant factors they may take into account in choosing between alternative solutions or deciding to deviate from the perfect quota.

In practice, despite disputes over their proposals, no one has seriously suggested that the commissioners have deviated from this pure and apolitical ideal. But the parties, in their claims and objections, have, of course, dressed up their self-interest in supposedly objective arguments about natural communities; they put together moving evidence of long-established links between particular localities for submission to the enquiries. But such efforts seem to make little impact.

The whole process of repeated enquiries can be long-winded and repetitive. The commissioners started work in 1976 and did not produce their final report until 1982. Since they were using 1976 electoral registration figures—(Britain has reasonably efficient compulsory registration)—there were some substantial anomalies by the time the proposals were implemented. Not all of these were due to the movement of population. Allowances for natural communities inspired the commissioners to continue the Isle of Wight with 95,000 electors as a single constituency while the constraints of London boundaries left Surbiton with only 48,000. Overall, only 74 percent of the English seats were within 10 percent of the quota. In Scotland the commissioners took pity on the difficulties of island travel allowing the Western Isles (24,000) and Orkney and Shetland

(31,000) to survive as single constituencies, while nearby Inverness had 67,000.[2]

The final proposals of the commissioners come into force only after an affirmative vote in Parliament. But the Westminster debates on the proposals are a farce. All sides accept that after a lengthy quasi-judicial process it would be absurd for the legislature to make amendments—and, granted the government's control of the House of Commons through strict whipping, any changes would be seen as partisan.

The general acceptance of the neutrality of the Boundary Commission is remarkable. Each postwar redistribution has, necessarily, favored the Conservative party because of the drift from city to suburbs. Moreover each redistribution has cost some prominent Members of Parliament (MPs) their seats.

The fact that the commission system works relatively well in Britain does not mean that it is a readily exportable device. In the United Kingdom, there is no requirement for MPs to live in their constituencies, and few politicians of stature, when redistricted out of one seat, have failed to find another. Local government units are more equal in size and few MPs have more than two or three local councils in their areas. It is possible to make a large proportion of constituency boundaries match with local boundaries, granted the widespread tolerance of a 10 percent or even a 20 percent variation in numbers. Moreover, the population is so distributed that there are few areas where there could be any question of adapting constituencies to serve ethnic or minority representation. Furthermore, despite a major lawsuit in 1982 (which failed abjectly), the whole issue cannot readily be made subject to litigation (and Britain, with no Bill of Rights, is a far less litigious place than the United States).

Britain may have pioneered the commission approach to redistricting, but it no longer provides the best example. All the other

---

[2] For historic reasons Scotland and Wales are overrepresented. It has been felt to be politically impossible to reduce the number of their seats, although their share of the United Kingdom's population has fallen. Their quotas at the last redistribution—53,000 and 58,800, respectively—were well below the English 65,700. Scotland has 72 seats when on a proportionate basis it should have only 57. Wales has 38 when it should have 32.

major democracies once ruled from the United Kingdom have single-member districts, and all now use impartial commissions for redistributing seats.

Australian boundary-drawing has always been done by commission, though in the past the process could be decidedly political in outcome if not in process. Incumbents' interests have sometimes been protected, and there used to be a provision for rural weighting. As recently as 1978, a minister was forced to resign for leaning on the commissioners over the name to be given to a seat. But the system has become increasingly less political.

Under the 1984 Electoral Act, the new Electoral Commissioner, Colin Hughes, an academic who had written widely on electoral systems, presided over a remarkable and total reapportionment. The 125 seats in the Lower House were redrawn into 148, with due judicial process, in a mere seven months. The commissioners in each state[3] were required to keep seats to within 10 percent of that state's electoral quota[4] as forecast by the census for three and one-half years hence (just halfway through the seven-year cycle for redistricting). Proposals were drawn up by the commissioners. Public inquiries were then held and in some cases led to modifications. Parliament was no longer allowed any discussion or vote on the proposals. The final outcome nationwide was generally welcomed. It could be shown that if either Labor or the Liberal/National Party coalition won 50.5 percent of the preferred vote they would almost certainly secure a majority of the seats.

At the state level in Australia reapportionment has not always been so noncontroversial. All states work through nonpartisan commissions composed of judges and officials, but there has been political interference. Moreover, in Queensland until 1990, a heavy rural loading was still preserved in the Western Australian Parliament and the Tasmanian Upper House (Hughes, 1985). It is worth stressing that it is only in the past twenty years that the Australian Common-

---

[3]Initially three public officials plus the federal election commissioner; later, to decide objections to their proposals, a federal judge and the federal statistician were brought in.

[4]Australia's redistricting is based on the registered electoral body, not on population. Australia's electoral registration system is very accurate.

wealth abandoned rural loading and that almost all the states moved to conform to the federal standards of equality of numbers and to ensure the independence of nonpartisan commissions. In New Zealand a representation commission has, since 1887, been responsible for redrawing boundaries every five years. Four of its eight members are public officials, such as the government statistician or the surveyor general, and there is a chairman who since 1956 has been a serving or retired judge; there are also two partisan members. In contrast to Britain or Australia the commission includes one government and one opposition nominee. Despite this, the neutrality of the commissioners is unquestioned. The Representation Commission is allowed to vary the size of electorates by up to 5 percent from the quotas established separately for the North Island and the South Island, and it is supposed to take account of existing boundaries, communities of interest, communication links, and topography. New Zealand politics has been so evenly balanced— (the elections of 1978 and 1981 were virtual ties)—that there has been great sensitivity about the political effects of redistribution, but (despite some complaints) the Commission's findings have been accepted as apolitical. As a quasi-judicial body its decisions are final and not subject to alteration by Parliament or by appeal to the courts (McRobie, 1987).

Canadians left their decennial federal redistricting to a committee of Parliament until the 1960s. The results were decidedly partisan. Pressure for reform grew and, consciously drawing on Australian experience, Parliament passed the Electoral Boundaries Readjustment Act (EBRA) of 1964. This placed the task firmly in the hands of electoral commissioners (now a three-person body drawn from judges, public officials, and academics). They are allowed to diverge by up to 25 percent from the provincial quota except in "extraordinary circumstances" when an even greater variation is permitted. In 1987 two-thirds of all seats were within 10 percent of the quota and only five out of the 29 seats went beyond the 25 percent limit of deviation. The commissioners, named anew after each decennial census, are required to report promptly; the House of Commons is entitled to debate the commissioners' proposals but it has no power to alter their maps. Changes to the EBRA in each decade have delayed the appointment of the commissions. As a result, boundaries based on the 1961 census only took effect in 1968; the 1971 census in 1979; and the 1981 census in 1988. Redistribution is always most painful when an area has to lose seats. In 1974 Canada met this problem when it adopted a "grandfather clause." In the future, no province would ever have its parliamentary representation reduced. This has necessitated a modest increase in the size of the House of Commons. The numbers rose from 265 in the 1960s to 282 in the 1970s and to 295 in the 1980s.

India has had three general redistrictings since independence. They have been carried out administratively by a statutory Delimitation Commission which deals with both national and state constituencies. In 1975, when there were fears that the energetic sterilization programs might reduce the representation of some states, it was agreed that there would be no further redistricting until the end of the century. This has led to vast discrepancies in population. Mainland constituencies in 1989 ranged from 1,600,000 in Outer Delhi to 30,000 in Lakshadweep. Only half the seats were within 15 percent of the quota. But the Delimitation Commission in 1957, 1963, and 1973 was not unduly worried about equal numbers. It allowed a wide tolerance in its efforts to respect established boundaries. Its proposals were not subject to changes in the Lok Sabha, and they do not seem to have excited much interest or pressure. In a very political country it is surprising that redistricting has been so little a source of political controversy.

Table 6.1 summarizes the redistricting pattern of the eight most significant long-established democracies with single-member districts. Countries have mostly used legislative districting throughout this century; it is only in the last generation that some have switched to the very pure and neutral arrangements which they now employ. Australia, now the most impeccably equal of systems, used rural loading well after *Baker* v. *Carr*, and within the last 25 years governments in both Britain and Canada have failed to give speedy effect to the commissioners' proposals, while in India routine redistricting was abandoned for political reasons. Yet there is no doubt of the sustained international trend toward keeping incumbent legislators out of the redistricting process and relying more on neutral commissions and stricter formal criteria such as population equality.

Almost all substantial democracies outside the Commonwealth use proportional representation with multimember or nationwide constituencies. Under most proportional systems, population movements can be dealt with by varying the number of seats in an area rather than by changing its boundaries. The problem of defining electoral districts becomes of negligible political significance. Ireland, with its three- and four-member constituencies using the single transferable vote, is one of the few exceptions (Mckee, 1983).

The two main examples of European countries with single-member districts are Germany and France. Under the German version of proportional representation, the Additional Member System, half the members of the Bundestag are chosen from single-member constituencies. But the drawing of their boundaries has caused little controversy because the seats allocated on the Länder (province) list will fully compensate for any partisan bias in the outcome in single-member seats. Boundaries are determined by a permanent seven-member constituency commission. It *should* not allow seats to deviate by more than 25 percent from the average population, and when deviations exceed 33.3 percent boundaries *must* be redrawn. Seats are allocated to the 16 Länder (provinces) in proportion to population and, as with states in America, it is a matter of Länd prestige not to lose seats. It is just possible by drawing boundaries ingeniously to increase a Länd's chance of getting an extra member of the Bundestag under the complications of the *uberhangsmandat* provisions of the proportional representation system. But this has hardly happened. The commission has to report within 15 months of each new Parliament. It is up to Parliament to give effect to its recommendations. This has been done punctually every four years since 1972.

In 1958 the Fifth French Republic reverted from the proportional representation system of the Fourth Republic to single-member districts and the second ballot. The districts were drawn up somewhat arbitrarily by the Ministry of the Interior. They were seen as broadly fair except for some deliberate attempts to limit Communist representation. Seats varied in population from 80,000 to 132,000. The 1958 boundaries were left unchanged for 28 years, and the anomalies of size had grown substantially by 1985 when France switched back to proportional representation.

Table 6.1 Cross-National Matrix

Nation	Model of Redistricting	Role of Legislature	Frequency of Redistricting	Electoral Surplus System	Seats in Legislature
Australia	Commission	None	7	Attended vote	148
Canada	Neutral commission	Can delay enactment	10	FPTP	308
France	Government	None	Nothing laid down	Second ballot	577
Germany*ᵃ*	Neutral commission	None	4	AMS (1/2 seek FPTP)	656
India	Neutral commission	None	10 years (suspended) (1976–2001)	FPTP	541
New Zealand	Neutral commission (with party reps)	None	5	FPTP	92
United Kingdom	Neutral commission	Normally formal but can delay enactment	15	FPTP	651
United States	Usually state legislature	Substantial	10	FPTP	435

(cont'd)

When single-member districts were restored in 1986 the process was again carried out by the Ministry of the Interior, but the minister was given guidelines by the Constitutional Council. The districts had to respect the boundaries of *departements*, and they had to be within 20 percent of the quota for the *departements*. Redistribution would take place after every second census.

For four months, from August to November 1986, the ministry proposals excited eager controversy among parliamentarians

Table 6.1   (*continued*)

Nation	Most Recent General Redistricting	Quota	Permitted Deviation	Litigation	Level of Political Controversy
Australia	1984	67,000 electors	10%	None	Now negligible
Canada	1988	87,000 population	25%	Some	Low
France	1988	108,000	20%	None	Negligible
Germany[a]	(W) 1988 (E) 1990	Population	33%	None	Low
India	1973	1,000,000 population	As equal as possible	None	Low
New Zealand	1987	34,000 population	5%	None	Medium
United Kingdom	1983	67,000 electors	As equal as possible	Some	Medium
United States	1982	600,000 population	Very small	A lot	High

[a] These figures for German scholars were modified by the merger with the West and in October 1990, the date of the last redistricting in West Germany. The number of seats is for the merged Germany.

and the political class. The Communists and the Socialists, as well as the National Front, complained of deliberate gerrymandering. The Socialists brought a case before the Constitutional Council. Terms familiar in American redistricting were used. Deputies and their districts were "collapsed," "exiled," "drowned," and "merged." An *ad hoc* commission of six judges, known as "sages," examined the proposals and raised questions about three-fifths of the *departements*. Some but not all of their objections were met in revised proposals. In the end, although President Mitterrand refused to sign the redistricting bill (on formal grounds), the Constitutional Council concluded that the final proposals accorded with the rules of fairness they had laid down. In the 1988 election (in which the Chirac government that had conducted the redistricting did not fare well) constituencies in metropolitan France varied from 26,300 to 71,400 electors.

The experience of 1986 in France is the most American of any major democracy with single-member seats. The majority party did try to draw boundaries in its own favor, but it was constrained by its own deputies seeking boundaries congenial to themselves as well as by the interventions of the *Commission des Sages*, the *Conseil d'Etat* (the Supreme Court for public law), and the *Conseil Constitutionel*.

What is notable about all these national approaches to the redistricting process is that none of them comes near to the rigor of the "one person, one vote" standard imposed in the United States since *Baker v. Carr*. New Zealand has the strictest rules, but it tolerates 5 percent deviations from the average. India, Canada, and the United Kingdom accept far greater deviations. There is a notable contrast between, on the one hand, the rigorous regard for numbers and the high politicization of the United States and, on the other hand, the more statistically relaxed approach but the lower politicization of the rest of the world.

Explaining Different Approaches

Why is the American approach to the problem of redistricting so vastly different from that of other countries? Clearly the American case is the aberrant one in that everywhere else, except France, the commission model has prevailed. Given the uniqueness of the American electoral system—most notably the weakness of its parties, the expense of its elections, and the locality rule among many aspects—one answer is that it would be surprising if the United States did *not* treat redistricting differently from other countries. A particular rule, practice, or institution in a country is necessarily affected by all its other rules, practices, and institutions. But that does not mean that what works well in one country cannot be exported to another. Can any useful lessons be learned about redistricting, or indeed electoral institutions generally, by studying the experience of other countries?

This question is particularly relevant to current debates over redistricting reform in the United States. Some Americans (including a few members of the Supreme Court, to judge by its recent decisions) are dissatisfied with the "political" approach to line-drawing and have pointed to the British or Australian style of commissions as a better alternative. They argue that it is possible to change constituency boundaries more impartially and that only the self-interest of politicians has prevented the adoption of basic reforms in the United States (Common Cause, 1977). Other Americans are highly skeptical of "neutral" commissions and fear that any attempt, however well-meaning, to give such commissions full power over redistricting would only make matters worse (Balitzer, 1979). They find it difficult to believe that British redistribution is truly neutral, just as the British are shocked by the idea that politics must play so major a role in American redistricting.

The gulf between such perceptions may never be closed. But it is relevant to the purpose of this book to explore why the United States and the Commonwealth countries differ so widely in their approach to redistricting and to identify the problems that would arise if the Commonwealth approach were to be tried in the United States.

1. Methods of Legislation

The legislative process differs widely between the United States and the countries of the Commonwealth. In a parliamentary system, backbenchers play a minor legislative role. The cabinet is responsible for policy initiatives. Backbenchers may, of course, ask questions of ministers, express their opinions in debate on the floor, and even defy the party whip when their differences with the leadership are unresolvable. To some extent, all of these tactics figure in the calculations of party leaders, but it is still a far cry from the decentralized legislative system familiar in the United States. Specialist committees in the House of Commons have been upgraded since the late 1960s, but they still lack the power to amend or delay bills. By contrast, specialist committees are extremely powerful in Congress and in state legislatures, and representatives routinely use their committee positions to defend the interest of their constituents. Presidents and governors cannot count on the strength of party ties to get bills through Congress—it is a process of continuous bargaining. As a consequence, many bills passed by Congress are really conglomerations of specific requests and log-rolled compromises.

In this light, it is not surprising that British (and Commonwealth) redistributions should exclude individual members from negotiations and that American redistricting should frequently include them. The idea that individual representatives should bargain over any bill, let alone a redistribution plan, would seem inappropriate in Britain. Conversely, the fact that legislators bargain over their seats is not as shocking to Americans, who daily observe Congress bargaining over everything else. The case that reformers in the United States must make is why redistricting should be treated differently from other kinds of legislation. If all bills in the national and state legislatures were shielded from the parochial interests of legislators, it is unlikely that the states would handle redistricting in the highly incumbent-oriented manner that they do now.

2. The Party System

Another major factor behind differences in the two types of redistricting practices lies in the contrast in party systems. If Britain were to switch to a more political approach to redistricting, it is likely that negotiations would be dominated by party interests to a greater extent than they are in the United States. This point overlaps with the first, of course, since parliamentary discipline is partly maintained by strong party ties as well as by structural factors, such as the hope of advancing to a cabinet career. Differences in the current practices also reflect the varying roles that the parties play in the two countries. Local British party organizations figure more significantly in the selection of members of Parliament than do their American counterparts. Campaign money is almost exclusively raised by the parties, and local activists run the election campaign. Representations to the Boundary Commission are therefore usually made by the local party organizations rather than by the members themselves. The Commission's emphasis on preserving previous constituency boundaries and communities of interest is compatible with the interests of the local parties, which naturally prefer minimal disruption to their organizations.

American parties have always been weak, and the reforms of the 1960s and 1970s in campaign finance and presidential selection have attenuated their influence even more. U.S. candidates raise their own money, develop their own campaign organizations, and owe far less of their support to normal party loyalty than do British candidates. The impact of redistricting plans on local party organizations is therefore a far less important issue in the United States. Rather, the central question in American redistricting is the effect that any proposed boundary changes will have on the incumbent's personal contributors and areas of highest support. This gives American redistricting a more idiosyncratic slant, with an inordinate emphasis on shopping centers, fundraising sites, and favorite neighborhoods.

3. Residence Requirements

Many U.S. state legislatures have a residence requirement stipulating that a person must reside in the district at the time that he or she files for candidacy. Congress does not have a formal residence requirement (except that the members must be residents of the state in which their district lies), but the informal expectations that a candidate should already have a residence in the district are so high that it is *de facto* compulsory. By comparison, the systems following the Westminster model have no formal residence requirement, and the informal expectation is far less strong. Only a minority of British MPs have had any long-established local connections when they were first selected. Winston Churchill represented Dundee, Manchester, and a London suburb during his career—and never had a house in his constituency; there is nothing unusual about such carpetbagging.

The effect of this is to make displacement a more important issue in American redistricting than it is in Britain. If an incumbent loses his seat in the United States, he cannot hope to run anywhere else in the country except in the immediate vicinity of the old constituency. A congressman from California cannot realistically consider the option of running for a seat in New York—he would be immediately branded as a carpetbagger. A displaced British MP need not restrict his options to the old locality and can without prejudice shop around for another constituency. Even when the local activists insist their candidate should reside in the constituency, this usually means that he should make himself available locally and take up residence if elected.

The residence expectation in the United States, like the weak parties and the decentralized legislative system, accentuates the emphasis on incumbency interest in American redistricting. By closing off the option of running in all but a few neighboring seats, the residence expectation raises the stakes of redistricting for incumbents who want to stay in office and makes them more resistant to changes dictated by demographic trends. If one party controls the process, the answer is usually to place the burden of displacement unequally on the other party. However, when this is not possible or when bipartisan agreement is necessary to pass a redistricting plan, other outlets for displaced legislators must be found—for example, opportunities to run for higher office, judicial appointments, and the like.

In Britain, incumbents have expressed distress when their seat is mutilated or destroyed by the boundary commissioners. But almost every politician of substance who has suffered thus has quickly found another seat, perhaps hundreds of miles away.

4. Differences in the Judicial Systems
The American judiciary is much more political in practice and in manner of appointment than the British judiciary. Many American judicial offices are elected, and even when they are not, the appointment is made by a political official (i.e., the president, senator, or governor) with an explicit eye toward the appointee's "judicial philosophy." In addition, judges in some states are subject to recall by statewide ballot.

British judges and barristers are largely removed from political pressure. Although they are in a traditionalist profession with conservative values, they are seldom involved in cases that affect political parties, or indeed, that raise constitutional questions.

The consequence of this difference is that Americans have good reason to be suspicious of those who claim that judges will act neutrally in these matters. The California Republican party lost every challenge that it made against the legislature's 1981–82 redistricting plan brought before a California supreme court that was controlled by Democratic appointees; this indeed spurred a major recall effort against three of the Democratic appointees to the court. In addition, it is significant that the commission initiative which the Republican party sponsored in the 1984 election purposely bypassed members of the state supreme court in favor of retired appellate judges (the majority of whom are registered Republicans). Whatever the objective merits of accusations about the California supreme court's political bias, it is an indisputable fact that the perception of partisan judicial bias has figured prominently in California's redistricting quarrels. By contrast, none of the British parties has ever impugned the integrity or neutrality of the Boundary Commissions, even though the results of redistribution have had more adverse consequences for Labour than for the Conservatives. In neither of the two substantial cases involving redistricting that have come before the High Court has anyone suggested that partisan considerations affected the judges' verdicts.

The suspicion of judicial partisanship and the willingness of U.S. courts to rule on specific cases and standards may also account for another crucial difference between U.S. and British redistricting practices—the American affinity for concrete and measurable standards. Standards that are complex and flexible are harder to apply and to defend. The inclination of the courts to use simple quantifiable criteria in an attempt to control more imprecise and controversial phenomena—like political gerrymandering—is nicely exemplified by the *Karcher* decision, in which the Supreme Court invalidated a New Jersey plan with less than 1 percent variance in favor of another one with even less variance. The Court made it clear that the real object of its concern was gerrymandering and that it thought that population equality—easy to measure and universally accepted as a goal—was a standard that it could use against politically unfair lines. This is demonstrably ludicrous, and as the Supreme Court entertains political gerrymandering cases in the future, it will be forced to find a more sophisticated standard or it will have to abandon the attempt to regulate vote dilution. Even so, it is safe to predict that in searching for such a standard the Supreme Court will be most attracted to simple, concrete tests—for example, compactness or a seats-votes ratio.

5. *Demographic Differences*

It is impossible to understand the relative importance of racial criteria in American redistricting as compared to Britain without taking into account the degree of ethnic diversity in these countries. The United States has substantial disadvantaged minority communities (10 percent black and 6 percent Latino). In addition, there are numerous less disadvantaged groups, such as Jews and Asians, who watch the consequences of redistricting very carefully. Britain's minority communities number less than 4 percent of the total population and, although concern has been widely expressed at the scarcity of black MPs, the idea that the problem could be solved by boundary drawing has not been seriously voiced. There are as yet virtually no areas where it would be possible to carve out a black constituency—and even where the minorities are strong, the divisions between Afro-Caribbeans and the rival groupings from the Indian subcontinent might well frustrate the election of a black MP.[5]

Even across states within the United States, it is clear that racial gerrymandering of both the positive and negative variety is an issue only in the states that have large ethnic minorities. A group must reach some critical size and concentration level before it needs to worry about the effects redistricting will have on its political influence. Thus, the Japanese-Americans, who are small in numbers and predominantly middle class and who have intermingled widely with the rest of the population, have not focused on redistricting strategies, whereas the blacks and Latinos, whose influence rests heavily on voter mobilization, have. While the size of the minority population determines whether racial gerrymandering will be an issue in a given state, the nature of the issue varies by region. The central question in northern and western states with large minorities has been positive racial gerrymandering (i.e., maximizing minority representation) while the issue in the South remains negative racial gerrymandering (i.e., attempts by the white majority to minimize minority representation). Moreover, it is clear that racial gerrymandering might not have become a judicial matter at all in

---

[5] In 1987 four nonwhite MPs were elected to the House of Commons, though none came from a constituency that was more than 45 percent nonwhite.

the absence of the Voting Rights Act of 1965 and the Court's civil rights decisions in the 1960s involving the Fourteenth and Fifteenth Amendments. Thus demographic diversity is a necessary but not sufficient condition for explaining the salience of racial issues. Obviously, historical development and regional factors matter as well. And the inevitable growth of minority populations in Britain and their concentration in certain city centers may make the creation of minority seats a real problem for the United Kingdom Boundary Commission when they next report in the mid-1990s.

6. Political Norms and Cultural Suppositions
How far norms and informal expectations support institutional arrangements and how far they follow from them is an old and irresolvable problem. No matter which position one prefers on this broad question, most would agree that both institutions and norms are stronger and more stable when they are consistent with one another than when they are not. American institutions are more fragmented, decentralized, and permissive of parochial interests. American political norms are more pluralistic, Madisonian, and tolerant of particularism. Americans on the whole expect different groups to lobby for their interests at all levels of government. Pluralist notions that authority should be fragmented and that coalitions of interests should be fluid but omnipresent are deeply ingrained in the American psyche. Actors in the political systems are not expected to be neutral or disinterested because the institutions are designed on the Madisonian premise that they are not. There is a degree of self-fulfillment in this system—people are, to some degree at least, what they are expected to be. If institutions expect and perhaps even encourage people to be self-interested and parochial, this no doubt dampens public-regarding actions. Political interactions are situations of cooperation, and if one group or individual acts in a public-regarding fashion while others act in a self-regarding fashion then the former are in danger of being made a "sucker" by the latter.

Political commentators have long noted that some segment of the American public periodically recoils from its pluralist, Madisonian roots. The Progressives sought to end machine politics by city manager reforms, nonpartisan ballots, and civil service reform. Revisionist historians have pointed out the value that these machines had in integrating immigrant groups into a hostile political environment and that many of the Progressive reforms strengthened the power of the middle class over disadvantaged groups. Their modern-day equivalents introduced campaign finance laws that were supposed to lessen the influence of money on politics. A decade later, Americans are painfully aware that this goal was not achieved and that instead it encouraged a proliferation of special interest political action committees (PACs). The experience with political reform in the twentieth century has only served to reinforce the cynicism of the American political culture.

The British political culture is less pluralistic and parochial. Burkean notions of representative independence and Whig ideas of functional representation, although modified by time, have given the British system a more coherent, ideological, and public-regarding cast. With the rise of party discipline and the demise of private member legislation in the nineteenth-century, the MP has had less opportunity and incentive to protect local, parochial interests. Groups such as unions or industrialists articulate their interests through a more disciplined and ideological party structure. Coalitions are more stable and appeals are made in a rhetoric that is less blatantly self-regarding.

British experience with institutional reform has been relatively positive. The nineteenth-century purification of the civil service and of the electoral system was notably successful. Cynicism about the political process may have grown in recent years, but there is still a remarkable residue of respect for the neutrality and objectivity of the senior figures in law and in administration. It is still possible to allay public anxiety about a problem by referring it to an independent committee drawn from the mandarins of Whitehall, the Inns of Court, and the universities.

The point is that the arrangements for redrawing boundaries in Britain and America are consistent with the general norms of the political culture. As a consequence, an American tends to view British redistribution practices as incredibly naive and dangerously trusting. If people were to act in self-regarding ways within the British rules, there would be tremendous latitude for injustice without the many avenues of appeal—court cases, recalls, and referendums—that exist in the United States. Given that most U.S. political actors normally act and are encouraged to act in self-regarding ways, there is a strong case for arguing that the British system would not work in the United States. Similarly, anyone brought up in the British tradition is likely to be puzzled by the fact that America cannot conduct its redistribution in a more rational, disinterested fashion; any attempt to adopt the political style of redistribution would seem inappropriate and would weaken public respect for the political system.

7. The Separation of Powers
The existence of a constitution interpreted by judges and implemented by an executive gives American legislators a freedom that might be unacceptable in a country with no written constitution and a sovereign parliament. Parliament can always override the courts and the courts have no power to disallow any law that Parliament may pass.

Americans know that for them the tyranny of a legislative majority will always be tempered, if not by the executive that carries out its laws then by the courts which decide whether they are consonant with the Constitution. In Britain, where one party dominates an omnipotent Parliament, it is far more urgent that those who have the power should show restraint about exercising it in a partisan way.

The idea that there must be a conflict of interest when MPs are judges in their own cases was recognized in 1870 when the House of Commons transferred jurisdiction over controverted elections to the courts. The collusive deals and inconsistent decisions that had characterized electoral disputes were done away with. A body of neutral case law was quickly established, and within a generation British elections had been transformed to an extraordinary degree. A similar code of ethics underlies Britain's commission approach to redistribution. In 1948 the Labour government carried through a redistribution that cost it 30 seats and, by denying it a working majority at the next election, barred the party from office during the affluent 1950s. In 1969, when another Labour government (with a plausible excuse about impending changes in local government boundaries) postponed implementing a new set of redistribution proposals, they provoked widespread indignation at this unilateral breach of fair play.

Lessons from Abroad

Americans have long looked to the British example for prospects of reform. The British party system provoked the responsible party movement in the United States. The success of the campaign expenditure laws in Britain helped to inspire the U.S. campaign finance laws of the mid-1970s. And now British redistribution is often touted as the answer to America's redistricting squabbles. It may be so, but the theme of this analysis is that institutions, like heart transplants, must be compatible with the environment to which they are moved. Just as human bodies reject foreign tissue, so institutions can be rejected or transformed beyond recognition if they are not properly modified before they are inserted. The new institution must be compatible with other institutions and the norms of the political culture.

The responsible party movement has floundered because there are too many alternative routes outside the party for would-be candidates to get themselves elected. U.S. parties do not control nomination, finance, or even manpower resources. In order for them to do so, there would have to be massive transformations in the laws governing primaries, spending, and party membership. Campaign finance reform cannot work until the United States is willing to restrict the principle of free speech from covering independent expenditure and to adopt a strict law of agency.

Redistricting reform parallels reforms in these other areas. If legislators are not subordinated to strong parties, their individual interests as incumbents will remain preeminent and will be expressed to commissioners in various ways. If there is no spending reform, attempts to use commissions to foster electoral competition will result in even more expensive elections. If the judiciary is not better insulated from political pressure, the perception of their neutrality will not be fostered. If the commission has open hearings and amends its plans upon public complaint, every special interest group will plead its case and lawyers in America will acquire yet another avenue of employment.

Lessons can be learned by studying electoral institutions comparatively, but they cannot be taken out of context. The questions that must be asked are how far does a particular institution exist independently and how much does it depend on other institutions and norms in the system? Institutional transplants may save the body politic if properly performed, but insufficient care to the surgical procedures can kill the patient.

Other democracies offer many useful examples worth studying by Americans. But for the improvement of redistricting processes it seems that the United States must look inward. Our next chapter explores possible reforms.

THE PATHS TO REFORM

The specter of new redistrictings and the bitter memories of old ones keep the debate over the need for redistricting reform alive. The belief that there may be a better way for the United States to redraw its district boundaries derives partly from the example of other democracies where, as the preceding chapter showed, independent, quasi-judicial procedures appear to offer relief from partisan and incumbent biases. The fact that most of these countries once used the legislative redistricting method and only recently abandoned it suggests that politicians can be persuaded to surrender their long-cherished authority in this area.

These comparative examples may seem alluring but, as the last chapter suggests, institutions and procedures that work well in other countries may not work as well when they are imported into the United States. Different conditions may cause the same rules or procedures to operate in unexpected ways in the American setting. Reformers have, however, proposed a number of plausible alternatives to current practices.

Confusions in the Dialogue over Reform

Two common confusions in the dialogue over U.S. redistricting reform can cause participants to talk past one another. The first concerns the appropriate standard for thinking about what is to be achieved. When some people discuss redistricting, they refer to the pragmatic political consequences of different procedures and

140

standards: Who gets political advantage if district lines are drawn in a particular manner or by a given process? This is the *realpolitik* perspective. Since all redistricting standards and procedures have a pragmatic and political dimension as well as an ethical dimension, it is easy to be cynical about any abstract discussion of reform. Compactness, for instance, may have certain desirable "good government" features, but it may also benefit one party or group more than another. To the political practitioner the real motive behind an ethical or "good government" argument is the pragmatic political one, and those who do not recognize this are naive.

At the opposite pole, there are those who fervently believe that redistricting should be considered from an ethical or "good government" perspective exclusively and that pragmatic political consequences have no proper place in the discussion. In its purest form, this position focuses on the rightness *per se* of a given procedure or standard, and intentionally disregards the political and representational consequences that might result. A good example is offered by the claim that legislative redistricting is unethical because incumbents who draw their own district lines have a conflict of interest. Even if legislative redistricting results in a plan that is widely accepted, it must be a bad process because the judgment of those who make redistricting decisions will be clouded by powerful and inappropriate considerations of self-interest.

A less extreme version of the ethical/"good government" perspective is more focused on controlling consequences by finding criteria that will produce a fair redistricting. It differs from a procedural ethics approach by judging the rightness of redistricting methods in terms of representational consequences rather than of due process *per se*, but it also differs from the pragmatic political perspective because it disregards specific political advantages and disadvantages and concentrates on broader issues of representation. The question is not which political party or group benefits from a given set of lines, but whether, for instance, districts should be made more or less competitive, or how the merits of minority representation should be valued against compactness.

Debates over redistricting reform always contain elements of each of these three arguments. Since advocates of each perspective

Table 7.1   Variations in Redistricting Perspectives

Perspective Type	Focus of Perspective	Example
1. Ethical rightness	Fairness of process or standards *per se*	A neutral method of line-drawing is morally required, whatever the consequences.
2. Ethical consequences	Fairness of electoral results under various districting proposals	The results under new district lines must be equitable, whatever the consequences.
3. Pragmatic political	Analysis of short-term political advantages	Compactness aids Republicans more than Democrats, or vice versa.

regard aspects of the other approaches as inappropriate, naive, or irrelevant, it is difficult to have a proper dialogue on the subject. What seems cynical and unethical to one appears realistic and plausible to another. The redistricting reform issue seems very simple to those who wish to disregard consequences and focus only on achieving the "right" process, and it seems complicated to those who look beyond procedural fairness as such to the actual geographic and political situation.

A second confusion burdening the discussion concerns the goals of reform. What is it that reformers want to achieve? Partisan gerrymanders, although rare, attract a great deal of attention and public outrage. One common reform goal, therefore, is to ensure that a majority party cannot use the redistricting process to gain advantage over a minority party. Partisan bias can mean either of two things, depending on which of the two notions of fairness discussed in

Chapter 3 is used as the basis of evaluation. If the standard is proportional fairness, then it means that one party has received a share of seats significantly above or below its share of votes. If the standard is seats–votes fairness, then the partisan bias means asymmetry in the seats–votes curve (i.e., a given share of the vote would not give the same number of seats to the Republicans as it would to the Democrats). The problem of bipartisan or incumbent gerrymandering is very different from that of partisan unfairness. A plan that benefits incumbents, creating as many safe seats as possible, necessarily diminishes the responsiveness of the relationship between seats and votes. As discussed on page 78, it is possible, at least in theory, to have a highly responsive system that is also symmetric (i.e., unbiased). It would not, however, also be proportional since small perturbations in the vote would lead to exaggerated changes in share of seats (Niemi, 1982; Browning and King, 1987).

Fairness as symmetry is a rather esoteric concept and one that is hard to implement in practice. Fairness as proportionality presents fewer difficulties. Therefore the latter is more widely accepted as a standard than the former; consequently, reformers are led toward the mutually exclusive goals of high responsiveness and greater proportionality rather than toward the logically more compatible pairing of high responsiveness and greater symmetry. This confusion leads to proposals that unrealistically promise to increase the number of districts that are competitive and that yield outcomes which are fair (i.e., proportional) to minority parties and to disadvantaged racial and ethnic groups. Confusions in language, in other words, often serve to hide the fact that redistricting involves real trade-offs and hard choices.

Options Assessed

Two categorical distinctions can help in classifying alternative redistricting approaches. The first, discussed in the previous section, is between procedures and standards. The second is between neutral and consensual goals. Neutrality means that rules and standards are impartial, while consensuality assumes high levels of agreement

Table 7.2   Alternative Ways of Reforming Redistricting

Type	Examples	Problems
Neutral procedures	Neutral agencies/commissions	Finding truly neutral line-drawers
	Randomizing procedures	Random procedures do not guarantee equitable results
Neutral criteria	Formal criteria (compactness, contiguity, equal population, etc.)	Need to rank the criteria; formal criteria do not guarantee equitable results
	Fairness formulae (proportional representation, symmetry, responsiveness, etc.)	Difficulties of measurement; nonproportional properties of SMSP system
Consensual procedures	Bipartisan commissions	Bias against challengers, minor parties, etc.
Consensual criteria	Supermajority voting rules	Possibility of stalemate
	Informal bargaining norms	Incentives for strategic manipulation

between all concerned. Four concepts then lie at the heart of the argument: neutral procedures, neutral criteria, consensual procedures, and consensual criteria. While the most natural pairings are between neutral procedures and neutral criteria and between consensual procedures and consensual outcomes, many actual reforms contain elements of three or more of these categories.

Neutral Procedures

The most frequently suggested reform is the creation of a nonpartisan redistricting body. At a minimum, this means taking responsibility for line-drawing out of the hands of the legislature and giving it to someone free from the conflicts of interest that all incumbents must face. There are a number of options in this direction. One, tried in Iowa and described on page 100, is to give the task to a nonpartisan agency, such as the Legislative Services Bureau. The critical question, of course, is whether such an agency can act with complete independence or whether it is really controlled by the legislative body which it is redistricting. As we saw, the problem with the Iowa Legislative Services Bureau has been that the redistricting plans which it formulates must ultimately be approved by the legislature. In countries with an independent civil service tradition and few political appointees, the option of giving the task to neutral civil servants or lawyers seems quite plausible, and it is likely that the agency's deliberations would be regarded as impartial. The U.S. civil service, however, is less independent than is the case in European or Commonwealth countries, and political appointees abound. Even when they do not, the agency depends on a budget controlled by the legislature. For these reasons, serious reform proposals in the United States seldom advocate a neutral civil service approach.

A second proposal, far more widely supported, involves the neutral commission. A neutral commission in the weakest sense is composed of individuals who are, at the very least, neither legislators or staff. A stronger version of a neutral commission would be one composed of disinterested and impartial individuals. Examples of weak neutral commissions can be found in Hawaii and Montana. Hawaii has a nine-person commission, eight of whom are appointed by the majority and minority leaders of both houses and the tie-breaking ninth member by the other eight. The Montana commission is similarly composed, but it only has five members. In both cases, the plans the commissioners develop become law without a vote of the legislature. This system avoids the conflict of interest objection but cannot be free from the suspicion of partisanship. Partisan viewpoints are intentionally balanced rather than excluded.

There are as yet no states that employ the strong version of the neutral commission proposal. However, a strong neutral commission proposal (the so-called Huening Initiative) was placed on the June 1990 California ballot and was only narrowly defeated. It proposed that twelve commissioners should be appointed by a panel of three retired appellate justices who would choose the names from a list put forward by nonpartisan, nonprofit public interest groups. No elected officials, their families or relatives, nor their staff members would be eligible. This commission would then review and decide between proposals submitted to it by outside groups, including the political parties or members of the legislature. Commissioners were to be barred from any conversations with affected parties outside the committee's deliberations. In 1984, Governor Deukmejian of California had proposed another strong version of the neutral commission idea which would have given the task to a board of retired appellate justices. This too was narrowly defeated by the California voters, 55 percent to 45 percent.

Why has the strong version of the neutral commission idea not been adopted in any of the states? And, in particular, why has it not been adopted in California, given the uproar created in 1981 by Phil Burton's plan and the state's historical proclivity toward reform experiments? Perhaps it is simply because partisan gerrymanders are too rare and bipartisan gerrymanders are too subtle. In the case of California, the Democrats may simply have hoodwinked the public with clever campaigns against reform measures, or the public may have been overwhelmed by the number of propositions on the ballot. However, it may also be that there is a deeply ingrained affinity toward the "pragmatic political" perspective in the American political culture which leads people to question whether truly neutral individuals can ever be found, or whether such individuals would remain impartial once they were placed in this position. Retired appellate justices, for instance, can be suspected of being beholden to the party that put them on the bench. Individuals nominated by nonpartisan, nonprofit groups may prove to be closet partisans. At least one strain of American political culture is deeply rooted in Madisonian skepticism about mechanisms that rely heavily on personal virtue; as a consequence, many Americans seem easily persuaded by the argument that truly neutral commissioners are hard to find or that the potential for abuse in systems that strive for impartiality is unacceptable. This may change, of course, if states like California or Indiana continue to have one divisive redistricting experience after another.

A third form of neutral procedures involves random redistricting mechanisms. The rationale behind this approach is this: If the process by which lines are drawn is random, then the proposed new districts cannot be intentionally partisan. The most common examples of random procedures involve automated computer design programs. In the 1960s, political scientists developed a number of programs that mechanically grouped contiguous census tracts into districts beginning at one corner of a state and moving in sequence to the bottom of the state. A variant of this, which has not yet been put on the California ballot (the Stanaland Initiative), would require that the redistricting begin in the upper northwest quadrant of the state and proceed laterally, picking up census tracts until it comes to the northeast border of the quadrant. Then the district drops down and picks up as many from the next row of tracts as are needed to fulfill the population quota. Of course, while randomness of this sort has the virtue of severely constraining the manipulation of district lines for partisan or bipartisan purposes, it also tends to create districts that violate city and county lines or that disregard the boundaries of significant ethnic and racial neighborhoods. Random impartiality is random with respect to both good and bad redistricting values. It may seem "right" to some because it effectively excludes malicious intent, but judged in terms of representational or pragmatic political consequences, randomness may unintentionally produce outcomes that are plainly undesirable.

The final type of neutral process is judicial. In a number of states (see p. 110), the courts are required to draw up redistricting plans if the legislature fails to do so. In 1973, for instance, the California state supreme court appointed a special master to draw district lines after Governor Reagan and the Democrat-controlled legislature were unable to come to an agreement. Had the Iowa legislature vetoed the Legislative Services Bureau's third bill and failed to produce its own solution, its 1981 redistricting would have been handed over to the state supreme court. As in the case of the impartial civil service option, a judicial approach makes more sense when the judiciary is insulated from partisan pressures. The judiciary in the United States is much more politically suspect because 36 of the 50 states elect their judges and in the remainder of the state and federal courts, appointments are controlled by elected officials. Perhaps for that reason, or because the courts have a well-developed instinct for self-preservation, the primary obstacle toward greater court involvement in the future lies in the courts' own reluctance. It is clear from its ruling in *Davis* v. *Bandemer* that the Supreme Court wants to be shown that there is serious abuse before it will intervene in such political matters. It also seems likely that lower and state courts will follow the Supreme Court's lead and continue to play the role of monitor or backup rather than accept control of the process.

Neutral Criteria

Whether a state uses some variation of the neutral procedure approach or not, it may want to shape redistricting outcomes by establishing neutral criteria. This in effect means setting forth impartial rules that redistricters must follow. If these criteria do not intentionally favor one party or group over another and if measures to assess how well districts conform to these standards can be developed, then it might not matter who draws the lines as long as they fall within an acceptable margin. This can be called the "handcuffs" approach to preventing gerrymandering: In theory, if there are enough neutral constraints, line-drawing cannot be intentionally manipulated to favor one group or party over another, regardless of who does the districting.

A number of these criteria were discussed in Chapter 2. They fall into two categories. First, there are aesthetic criteria—compactness, contiguity, equality of population, respect for city and county boundaries, and respect for natural features such as mountains, rivers, forests, and oceans. Some of these criteria may have independent representational value. For instance, compactness may facilitate contacts between representatives and constituents. It could be plausibly argued that when areas within a district are geographically remote, the chances of being visited by a representative will be small. Or, quite possibly, districts that respect natural boundaries and topological features may compose a more natural community of interest. People on the coast, for instance, may have a common interest in offshore oil drilling, while those living near forests may care intensely about logging issues; people in rural areas may have common interests that need protection from the urban majority. Quite apart from the independent value of these criteria, many reformers argue that the imposition of enough aesthetic standards will prevent gerrymandering. In theory, redistricters would be sufficiently "handcuffed" by these rules to prevent them from manipulating district lines to the advantage of one party or group over another. Compact, equally populated, contiguous districts that respect real communities of interest may unintentionally hurt some groups and benefit others, but at least the lines could not be purposely contorted for partisan or racial advantage (Baker, 1989; Grofman, 1985b).

Two arguments have become central in the debate over the strength of this approach. Some question whether aesthetic criteria can be truly neutral. Lowenstein and Steinberg, for instance, have argued that compactness favors the Republican party because Democratic neighborhoods are densely concentrated in inner-city areas (1985). A compactness requirement, they maintain, will legitimize Republican efforts to pack (i.e., concentrate) Democratic voters into a smaller number of districts. Their conjecture remains unproven, but it does raise an interesting question: If a redistricting standard or rule affects a particular group in an adverse manner, is it still neutral? Since it is possible to examine the likely effects of a proposed standard prior to its adoption, and since it is quite possible that many of them do affect groups in different ways, it may be impossible to persuade those adversely affected by a given standard that it is in fact neutral. Attempts to restrict "pragmatic political" considerations from the discussion, as we said earlier, are usually unsuccessful in American political culture. It is like trying to force people back behind the Rawlsian "veil of ignorance" after they have already stood in front and looked. Political innocence, once lost, cannot be easily reclaimed. Thus one difficulty with neutral criteria returns to the differing and conflicting ways that people evaluate reform proposals (which may be crudely categorized as nonconsequentialist ethical, consequentialist ethical, or pragmatic political).

The other and related concern about aesthetic criteria is whether they do indeed effectively "handcuff" potential gerrymandering. If these criteria have different effects on different groups and if these effects are known in advance, the potential for mischief in the name of neutrality is substantial. This is especially a problem when tradeoffs have to be made between separate and conflicting criteria. If compactness, for instance, conflicts with natural communities of interest, the party in charge of redistricting may choose the weighting of these considerations that most benefits its own interests. Moreover, since there is no necessary connection between what districts look like and the fairness of outcomes that result from them, the criteria may be used to justify results that benefit some groups over others.

This has led some political scientists to a second neutral standard approach: the application of some seats–votes formula. As our earlier discussions of proportional and neutral seats–votes ratios showed, districting plans could be required to produce outcomes that measure up to one or the other of these formulas. Thus, if proportionality is the standard, the plan that produces the most proportional outcome would be adopted, or if the standard is a neutral seats–votes curve, the one with the lowest bias and/or highest responsiveness would be chosen.

While this is intuitively appealing to many political scientists, neutral formula approaches have not achieved much acceptance for several reasons. For instance, it is difficult to say conclusively what the electoral effects of a districting plan will be before an election is actually held, and it is even harder to project back into the past to say what the outcome might have been had a different set of lines been in operation during the preceding election. In short, these measures depend upon counterfactual projections about what might happen in the future or what would have happened in the past under different districting arrangements. The techniques of election projection are so crude, and the idiosyncratic, hard-to-predict components of American elections are so important, that it is difficult to have great confidence in them. This places the redistricters and eventually the courts in the awkward position of choosing one set of district lines over another on the basis of shaky empirical information. Another problem with the seats–votes formulas is that there is no current consensus in the United States about which should be adopted. Traditionally, single-member, simple plurality systems were not expected to yield proportional outcomes. Rather, the appropriate standard was a neutral seats–votes curve. However, a growing number of electoral groups in the United States seem to equate fair outcomes with proportional outcomes. Since proportional and neutral seats–votes standards can conflict, a state or local political unit would have to decide which of these it wanted to adopt. It might not find that easy.

Consensual Procedures

Consensual procedures, unlike neutral ones, do not strive for objective impartiality (Dixon, 1981; Cain, 1984). Rather, the best outcomes are those that enjoy the highest level of support. The higher the threshold level of consent necessary, the higher the legitimacy of a law or procedure. A consensual process may or may not be impartial. All that can be said for certain is that whatever it produces must receive a high level of support.

The point of a consensual redistricting process is to make sure that as many as possible of the affected parties consent to the new district lines. There are a number of possibilities. One is to require a supermajority vote from the legislature or commission that has been given the redistricting task. Several states currently require a two-thirds vote on legislative redistricting bills (Maine and Connecticut were pioneers in this); this means, in effect, that no plan can be imposed on the minority party without its consent. In the state of Washington, a five-person redistricting commission draws the lines and submits them to the legislature for a two-thirds vote. New York requires that any plan submitted by its legislative task force must be passed as a joint resolution of the state legislature. These mechanisms virtually eliminate the prospect of partisan gerrymandering (i.e., bias in the seats–votes curve), but at the same time they tend to encourage bipartisan or incumbent-oriented plans (i.e., low responsiveness in addition to low bias).

A second consensual approach is to create an explicitly balanced commission—that is, instead of a commission composed of nonpartisans, one composed evenly of partisans. Connecticut, for instance, provides for a nine-person redistricting commission to be established if the legislature fails to come up with a plan that passes. The major parties get four appointments each, with the ninth elected by the other eight. Similarly, the five-person Washington state redistricting commission consists of members appointed by each of the leaders of the state legislature's party caucuses. The Hawaii and Montana commissions, discussed earlier, are also bipartisan in the sense that the majority and minority leaders are given equal shares of the commission appointments. Some states (e.g., Maine) have bipartisan advisory commissions, whose recommendations can be amended by the legislatures. Others provide for bipartisan backup commissions that come into operation if the legislature fails to enact a plan by a given date. And finally, other states use bipartisan commissions for state legislative districting but not for congressional districting (e.g., New Jersey). While bipartisan composition is a common feature of redistricting commissions, it is not universal. Indiana, for instance, has provided for a backup commission that consists of a representative from the governor, the majority leaders and the chairpersons of the redistricting committees in the two state legislative houses, all of whom could in theory belong to the same party.

Most recently, in 1990, Californians rejected two ballot propositions with different kinds of consensual mechanisms. Proposition 118 would have required a two-thirds majority in the legislature for any redistricting bill, just as is required in California for budget votes. The other, Proposition 119, would have required a supermajority vote of a twelve-person commission composed of five members from each of the two largest parties and two independent members. The consensual aspect of these proposals was not a major factor in their defeat. Instead, the controversy focused primarily on the nearly identical list of "neutral" criteria, the "handcuffs" that the legislature in Proposition 118 (and the commission in Proposition 119) would have had to use.

For most states, consensual procedures are unnecessary. The single greatest reason why partisan gerrymandering is so rare and bipartisan consensus is so common in the United States is that bipartisan agreement is necessary in a legislative redistricting when neither party has complete control of the process. In short, the most important consensual mechanism may be split control of state government. If at least one of the state legislative houses or the governorship is in different hands, the effect will be similar to a two-thirds vote requirement or to an evenly balanced commission.

Consensual Criteria

Consensual rules are commonly used in redistricting but are rarely written down. They evolve informally out of bipartisan redistricting negotiations. Most commonly, they are norms of sharing. For instance, if districts have to be added or collapsed because of population surpluses or deficits, it is common to expect an even division with half of the new seats going to each party or with changes being made proportionately to the share of over- or underpopulated areas controlled by each party. These rules are similar to Schelling's implicit bargaining points. Due to a common ethical tradition, evenness and proportionality seem like fair bargaining strategies to many Americans.

A second sort of consensual rule is akin to Occam's razor— that is, unnecessary changes should be minimized. The *status quo* is preferred for a variety of reasons (some selfish, some not) and departures from it are only justified by legal or demographic necessities. This norm often causes some public frustration because people have a tendency to judge their responsibilities for accepting change on the basis of their specific situation exclusively, rather than from the perspective of the overall statewide situation. Thus local officials look at their city or county populations and conclude that their obligations can be inferred from that statistic alone: If their city or county has enough population for one district, then it should not be divided into two or more districts; alternatively, if the existing district in that area needs only 10,000 people to bring its population up to the ideal, then it should add only 10,000 people. In reality, changes in one corner of the state have implications throughout the state due to the "ripple effect." So the true measure of necessary change requires information about the entire state. Only after that information is discovered can the doctrine of minimal change be implemented.

There are also a number of more idiosyncratic consensual rules that develop in the course of negotiations. For instance, legislators in one house often defer to the other house when it comes to the other house's district lines. In return, they expect reciprocal deference for their own district lines. Sometimes, too, there are unspoken rules about each legislator's bottom line. In other words, everyone is allowed to declare some portion of their district as inviolable so that changes are restricted to nonessential areas. Another example of a consensual understanding is a limit on population displacement in the amount of new territory a district must absorb. There are also common expectations about who should bear the brunt of redistricting changes, based on the relative seniority of various legislators or their relative popularity.

None of these consensual norms are ever codified in state constitutions in the way that neutral criteria are. However, they are frequently employed in redistricting negotiations and are essential to bipartisan outcomes. While it might serve no purpose to formalize them, it is important to recognize that informal rules of fairness may be as critical to what is perceived to be a "fair" redistricting as formal rules.

An Overview

There will never be a perfect, noncontroversial answer to the problem of redistricting. Overseas, Australia offers a model of how one country tried to remove the process from politics. But as we have argued, the Australian procedures could not easily be adapted and accepted within the American political culture. In the United States, however, despite diversity and controversy, the situation is one that has vastly improved over the past generations. Since *Baker* v. *Carr* all of the most gross anomalies have been squeezed out of the system by legislative enactment or by court order. Partisan ingenuity can still devise constitutionally acceptable boundaries that marginally favor one party or ethnic group, but compared to the boundaries that existed thirty years ago, the ability to alter electoral outcomes is much less.

In the 1990s, the critical issue will be the meaning of vote dilution. If what is meant by an undiluted vote is increasingly defined as proportional representation for parties and groups, the single-member district system used for congressional elections will be severely tested. States that opt for neutral procedures alone may find that this pleases neither affected political interests nor the courts. Also, the usual ordering of neutral criteria may have to change, with fairness formulas becoming more important and formal values like compactness and respect for local government jurisdictions becoming less important.

In the end, however, the single-member, simple plurality district system is not the best way to achieve proportional fairness. The thrust of the equity revolution in voting rights may ultimately undermine support for the traditional system for electing Congress. In the short run, states may try to use creative redistricting arrangements to assuage groups that want greater representation, but this may not prove to be enough. If so, the failure of redistricting to create political fairness may lead to the ultimate abandonment of our single-member, simple plurality system for electing Congress.

GLOSSARY

Additional Member System (AMS). The proportional system used in Germany. Half the members are elected by first-past-the-post voting in single-member constituencies. The other half are allocated to party lists in such a way that the seats in the full assembly are proportionate to the votes cast in the country as a whole (subject to certain threshold rules).

Affirmative action. A policy to ensure proportionate, or more than proportionate, representation for hitherto underrepresented minorities.

Aggregate fairness. The extent to which any local deviations from balanced redistricting cancel out so that, as a whole, no party or grouping is disadvantaged.

Alabama paradox. Under the formula used for the allocation of seats to states from 1910 to 1940 it was possible for a seat that gained in population to lose representation. This occurrence is known as the Alabama paradox.

Alternative vote (AV). Preferential voting within single-member constituencies. For the Australian lower house, for example, every elector is required to number all the candidates in order of preference; the candidate with fewest first preferences is eliminated and higher second preferences are counted instead; the process continues until one candidate has a clear majority.

Apportionment. The process of allocating congressional districts across states.

At-large. When one or several members are elected by the whole of a state or by the whole area of a local authority they are described as being elected at-large.

Bipartisanship. Occurs when the rival parties agree on the procedure and substance of redistricting. It is possible to have a "bipartisan gerrymander" when the parties mutually agree to preserve or increase the safety of the seats of incumbent representatives.

Blindfold redistricting. The drawing of boundaries by some general formula which has no regard to specific party or incumbent interests.

Building block. The basic minimum unit used in drawing up boundaries. It could be as large as a county but is now usually a census district or even a census tract.

Census block; Census tract. Areas designated by the Census for the collection and presentation of data.

Commission. A statutory and independent body charged with researching or implementing policy. Boundary commissions have been used widely in the English-speaking world so that constituencies can be delineated without direct political interference.

Community. A geographic grouping of the population with common interests dictated, for instance, by local government boundaries, transport or school facilities, ethnicity, language, or simply tradition.

Compactness. Having the minimum distance between all the parts of a constituency (a circle or a hexagon is the most compact district). Compactness is seen as one of the main defenses against gerrymandering.

Competitive seats. A seat where the margin of victory is small enough to make a change of control possible. *See* **Marginal seats**.

Constituency. The most common term for the geographic areas into which a country is divided for electoral purposes. A constituency may send one or several members to the legislature. Other terms include district (United States), riding (Canada), circonscription (France), electorate (Australia and New Zealand), and division (U.K.).

Contiguity. All parts of a district being connected at some point with the rest of the district.

Cracking. A term used when the electoral strength of a particular group is excessively dispersed by a districting plan.

Cube Law. A formula used to describe the way in which first-past-the-post systems exaggerate majorities in votes into much greater majorities in seats. If votes are divided in the ratio A:B, seats are likely to be divided in the ratio $A^3:B^3$.

Delimitation. Redistricting in India.

Dispersed minority. An ethnic or cultural minority that is not concentrated in a single area, where it could expect to control representation.

Displacement. The number of constituents added to or subtracted from a seat by a redistricting proposal.

District. In the United States, a legislator's constituency.

Electorate. The members of the population entitled to vote. Sometimes used for the eligible population and sometimes for those actually registered. In Australia "electorate" is often used as a synonym for constituency.

Ethnic fairness. Constituencies drawn to ensure due representation for ethnic minorities.

Ethnic voting. Voting for representatives coming from one's own ethnic group.

Fairness. A term used in many different ways to describe the ideal goal of redistricting—the drawing of boundaries that give no undue advantage to any party, region, or group.

First-past-the-post (FPTP) system. The oldest kind of voting arrangement, still predominating in English-speaking countries. It usually involves single-member districts. Each elector has one vote, and the candidate who gets most votes wins, even if he does not secure an absolute majority. Also known as the relative majority or plurality system.

Gerrymander. The drawing of constituency boundaries deliberately to secure party advantage.

Huntingdon formula. Devised in 1940 by Professor Huntingdon, a formula for the allocation of seats to states in as just a fashion as possible, avoiding the Alabama paradox.

Incumbency effect. The tendency of districts to re-elect an incumbent representative.

Linear ripples. The consequence of changing the boundaries of one district so that several others are necessarily affected.

Majority minority districts. Term used by the courts for seats where an ethnic minority constitutes a majority of the population.

Malapportionment. Condition when districts are poorly or disproportionately drawn, creating inequitable representation.

Marginal seats. Seats where the past voting record suggests a high possibility of change in party control. The term is sometimes used for seats where the last margin of victory was under 10 percent.

Metes and bounds. Detailed street-by-street descriptions of district boundaries.

Natural boundaries. District boundaries dictated by natural geographic features.

Open seat. A district in which the incumbent is not standing again.

Overrepresentation. Condition when a state or region or group elects more members than its population would entitle it to on a proportionate basis.

Overage. The excess population of a district, over the ideal population.

Overall range. The sum of the largest deviations above and below the average or quota for district size.

Packing. Compressing the electoral strength of a particular group into one constituency by a districting plan.

Partisan skew. The extent to which one party is advantaged by the drawing of boundaries.

Plurality. Another word for majority, but implying that the victor in an election has more votes than any other candidate, not that he has more than 50 percent.

Proportional representation (PR). Generic term for all the systems of election that seek, by multimember seats or reserve lists, to relate seats to votes more proportionately than is possible under a single-member constituency system.

Quota. The number of electors (or the population) that a district should contain on the basis of exact equality between districts.

Reapportionment. The allocation of seats to states.

Redistribution. British term for two processes distinguished in American usage: "redistricting" and "reapportionment."

Redistricting. The drawing of constituency boundaries.

Registration. The process of putting eligible citizens on an electoral register, entitling them to vote.

Responsiveness. A system in which small changes in the percentage of votes produce relatively large changes in the share of seats.

Ripple effect. The way in which a change in one district's boundaries necessarily affects the boundaries of adjacent districts and then of districts still farther away.

Risk-averse strategies. Redistricting carried out in a way designed to preserve the interest of incumbents.

Rural loading. Redistricting in which rural areas have smaller electorates than urban ones.

Safe seats. Seats where the margin of victory is so great that even a large swing would not oust the incumbent.

Second ballot. System used in the Third and Fifth Republic France, under which, in a single-member constituency system, there is a second vote a week after the first one, if no candidate has an absolute majority. It is analogous to the run-off arrangements in some American primary elections and is known as the exhaustive ballot when it is allowed to continue to a third or fourth ballot to secure a clear majority.

Single-member district. District electing only one representative.

Single-transferable vote (STV). System of proportional representation, used in, for example, Ireland.

Standard deviation. A statistical formula to measure variance from a norm; for example, dispersion of constituency sizes from the national or statewide mean.

Symmetry. Absence of any party bias in the relation of seats and votes.

Threshold. A statutory or practical minimum number of votes that a party must receive before it gets even one seat.

Underrepresentation. An area or grouping that has less representation than its numbers would entitle it to on a strictly proportionate basis.

Undercounting. The failure of the census to record the full population of an area.

Vinton method. Formula used from 1841 to 1910 to allocate seats to states after each decennial census.

Wasted votes. Votes contributing nothing toward the election of a representative.

LEADING CASES

Wood v. *Brown*, 287 U.S. 1,8 (1932)

A Mississippi law that created congressional districts of unequal population was upheld by the Supreme Court. Four justices underscored the Court's hands-off attitude by suggesting that it did not have jurisdiction over redistricting.

Colegrove v. *Green*, 328 U.S. 549 (1946)

This case challenged the redistricting in Iowa, which created unequal population districts (ranging in size from barely 100,000 to more than 300,000). But with a decision of 4–3, the Supreme Court refused to intervene, arguing that redistricting was a "political thicket" that the courts should avoid.

South v. *Peters*, 339 U.S. 276 (1950)

Georgia's county unit system of primaries for state elections heavily discounted urban voters (predominantly black), making their votes sometimes 1/120 of another county's votes. The Supreme Court upheld the dismissal of this case, refusing to exercise their equity powers in cases that pose political issues arising from a state's geographic distribution of electoral strength among its political subdivisions.

Gomillion v. *Lightfoot*, 364 U.S. 339 (1960)

Supreme Court decided to enter the "political thicket" of *Colegrove* by striking down the Alabama legislature's attempt to redraw the city boundaries of Tuskegee to exclude virtually all black voters.

Baker v. *Carr*, 369 U.S. 186 (1962)

In a landmark 6–2 decision, the Supreme Court decided the federal judiciary had the power to review the apportionment of state legislatures, and thus by implication, congressional redistricting. The case involved the apportionment of the Tennessee General Assembly.

Wesberry v. Sanders, 376 U.S. 1 (1964)
The one person, one vote standard was here applied by the Supreme Court to congressional districts. It struck down a Georgia map that had not been changed since 1931, featuring a population disparity of 550,000 between the most and least populous districts. This decision caused nearly every state for the rest of the decade to redraw its congressional district lines.

Reynolds v. Sims, 377 U.S. 533 (1964)
The Supreme Court decided that seats in both houses of a bicameral state legislature must be apportioned on a population basis, the aim being fair and effective representation.

Burns v. Richardson, 384 U.S. 73 at 88 (1966)
The Supreme Court ruled that the Equal Protection Clause does not necessarily require all districts to be single-member.

Avery v. Midland County, Texas, 390 U.S. 474 (1968)
The Texas Supreme Court determined that selection of the county commissioners court from single-member districts of substantially unequal population did not violate the Fourteenth Amendment. However, the Supreme Court ruled that the federal Constitution permits no substantial variation from an equal population in drawing districts for units of local government having general governmental powers over the entire geographic area served by such a power, and the case was remanded.

Kirkpatrick v. Preisler, 394 U.S. 526 (1969)
A Missouri plan of congressional redistricting that had a disparity of approximately 6 percent between the most and least populous districts was struck down by the Supreme Court, 6–3. The Court established that the state must provide substantial evidence of the unavoidability of variation in order to allow any deviations from "one person, one vote" application of redistricting.

Wells v. Rockefeller, 394 U.S. 542, 554–5 (1969)
A New York redistricting plan that created congressional districts of nearly equal population within regions of the state, but not

of equal population throughout the state, was rejected by the Supreme Court.

Gaffney v. Cummings, 412 U.S. 735 (1973)
The Supreme Court upheld the state legislature's consideration of "political fairness" between major political parties when drawing legislative districts. (The plan in this case had taken into account voting in the last three statewide elections.)

Mahan v. Howell, 410 U.S. 315 (1973)
The majority of the Supreme Court held that states have some leeway to deviate from the "equal-population principle" in apportioning districts in either or both houses of their legislatures if that variation is based on "legitimate considerations incident to the effectation of a rational state policy." "Respect for boundaries or political subdivisions" was considered one such reasonable basis.

Salyer Land Co. v. Tulare Lake Basin Water Storage District, 410 U.S. 719 (1973)
The Supreme Court upheld the district court's decision, saying that the California statute limiting voting for board of directors for the water storage district to landowners and excluding tenants of farmland within the district does not violate the equal protection clause and is constitutionally valid, since the legislature could have felt that there was a difference in interest between landowner and tenant.

White v. Regester, 412 U.S. 755 (1973)
A Texas congressional districting plan which calls for the largest disparity of 9.9 percent, but an average disparity of 1.82 percent, was ruled as unacceptable by the Supreme Court. The Court held that although the plan was not invidiously discriminatory, the disestablishment of two multimember districts into single-member districts was justified because of the history of discrimination against blacks and Mexican-Americans residing there. The state's argument that the disparity was an acceptable result of an attempt to avoid political subdivisions was also rejected under the strict application of the "one person, one vote" doctrine.

Chapman v. Meier, 420 U.S. 1, 95 (1975)
For North Dakota's reapportionment of the legislative assembly, a three-judge district court adopted a permanent reapportion-

ment plan which involved five multimember senatorial districts and contained a population variance of 20 percent between the largest and smallest districts. The Supreme Court held that, absent persuasive justifications, a court-ordered reapportionment plan of a state legislature must avoid the use of multimember districts and must ordinarily achieve the goal of population equality with little more than *de minimis* variation. The Court held that the burden of proof lay on the reapportioning court, and since it failed to articulate such persuasive justifications, the plan was rejected.

Connor v. Finch, 431 U.S. 407 (1977)

In the reapportionment of the Mississippi legislature, the Supreme Court rejected the final reapportionment plan, holding that the plan ordered by the district court for Mississippi's Senate and House of Representatives failed to meet the most elemental requirement that legislative districts be "as nearly of equal population as is practicable." The plan's maximum population deviations were as high as 16.5 percent in the Senate districts and 19.3 percent in the House districts. The Supreme Court also charged the district court to either draw legislative districts which are reasonably contiguous and compact, so as to put to rest the suspicions that black voting strength is being purposely diluted, or explain precisely why in a particular instance that goal cannot be accomplished.

Mobile v. Bolden, 446 U.S. 55 (1980)

In this racial, multimember district case, the Supreme Court put forward the "discriminating purpose test" for violations of the Equal Protection Clause—later used to deal with political gerrymandering.

Ball v. James, 451 U.S. 355 (1981)

The constitutionality of an Arizona statute providing that voting for directors of an agricultural improvement and power district was limited to landowners, with votes essentially apportioned to owned acreage, was challenged by the registered voters who owned either no land or less than one acre. The Supreme Court held that, similar to the argument in *Salyer*, the "one person, one vote" principle was not invoked, because the role of the directors was still rather narrow and the majority of the decisions affected the landowners only.

Karcher v. Daggett, 426 U.S. 725 (1983) (or 103 S.Ct. 2653)
By a 5–4 vote, the Supreme Court rejected a New Jersey congressional district map that called for a variation of 0.7 percent between the most and least populous districts. In doing so, the Court stressed that states must prove the variations are necessary to achieve some legitimate goal, but otherwise, there is no uniform level of population disparity that is tolerable.

Ketchum v. Byrne, 740 F.2d 1398 (7th Cir, Ill.) (1984)
Black and Hispanic residents of Chicago brought action challenging an aldermanic ward redistricting plan. The Supreme Court held that Chicago's redistricting plan indeed violated the Voting Rights Act and the court-approved redistricting plan did not grant minority citizens a reasonable and fair opportunity to elect candidates of their choice.

Thornburg v. Gingles, 478 U.S. 30 (1986)
The Supreme Court ruled that six multimember legislative districts in North Carolina violated the Voting Rights Act of 1982 because they impermissibly diluted the strength of black voters. The Court ruled that regardless of the lawmakers' intent, a voting system that has the effect of discriminating against minorities is in violation of the law.

Davis v. Bandemer, 478 U.S. 109 (1986)
Although the Supreme Court decided that the GOP-drawn legislative map in Indiana did not constitute a partisan gerrymander, it declared that partisan gerrymanders were legally challengeable.

Badham v. Eu, 694 F.Supp. 664 (N D Cal) (1988)
The Supreme Court ruled that a Democratic-drawn congressional district map in California did not constitute an unacceptable partisan gerrymander. The Court thus left undefined what would be an unacceptable partisan gerrymander.

Garza v. County of Los Angeles (1989)
A federal district court judge in Los Angeles ruled that the Los Angeles County Board of Supervisor had violated the Voting Rights Act by gerrymandering its districts in order to dilute the Hispanic vote. A few months later, he approved a new map which

included a newly created supervisorial district with a majority of Hispanics.

Board of Estimate v. *Morris*, 57 U.S. LW 4357 (1989) or 109 S.Ct. 1433

The Supreme Court ruled New York City's complicated scheme for selecting the powerful Board of Estimate as unconstitutional. Among other things, this process provided for one member from each of the city's boroughs regardless of their population, and also provided for a weighted voting system, giving some members more power than others.

BIBLIOGRAPHY

Books

Baker, Gordon E. *The Reapportionment Revolution.* New York: Random House, 1967.

Balinski, Michael L. and H. Peyton Young. *Fair Representation: Meeting the Ideal of One Man, One Vote.* New Haven: Yale University Press, 1982.

Balitzer, Fred. *The Commission Experience: Studies of Non-Legislative Approaches to Redistricting.* Claremont, Calif.: Rose Institute of State and Local Government, November 1979.

Bogdanor, V. and David Butler. *Democracy and Elections.* London: Cambridge University Press, 1983.

Bork, R. H. *The Tempting of America.* New York: The Free Press, 1990.

Cain, Bruce E. *The Reapportionment Puzzle.* Berkeley: University of California Press, 1984.

California Redistricting. Claremont, Calif.: Rose Institute of State and Local Government, 1980.

Common Cause. *Toward a System of "Fair and Effective Representation."* Washington, D.C.: Common Cause, 1979.

Congressional Quarterly's *Guide to U.S. Elections,* 2nd Ed. Washington, D.C.: Congressional Quarterly Inc., 1985.

Davidson, Chandler, ed. *Minority Vote Dilution.* Washington, D.C.: Howard University Press, 1984.

de Grazia, A. *Apportionment and Representative Government.* Washington, D.C.: American Enterprise Institute for Public Policy Research, 1963.

Dixon, Robert. *Democratic Representation; Reapportionment in Law and Politics*. New York: Oxford University Press, 1968.

Fenno, Richard. *Home Style: House Members and Their Districts*. Boston: Little, Brown, 1978.

Fiorina, Morris. *Congress: Keystone of the Washington Establishment*. New Haven: Yale University Press, 1977.

Forster, Lorn S., ed. *The Voting Rights Act: Consequences and Implications*. New York: Praeger Publishers, 1985.

Frantzich, Stephen E. *Computers in Congress: The Politics of Information*. Beverly Hills: Sage Press, 1982.

Goldwin, Robert A., ed. *Representation and Misrepresentation; Legislative Reapportionment in Theory and Practice*. Chicago: Rand McNally, 1968.

Grofman, Bernard; Lijphart, Arend; Mckay, Robert; and Scarrow, Howard, eds. *Representation and Redistricting Issues*. Lexington, Mass.: Lexington Books, 1982.

Hacker, Andrew, ed. *Congressional Districting; The Issue of Equal Representation*. Washington, D.C.: Brookings Institute, 1964.

Hardy, Leroy; Heslop, Alan; and Anderson, Stuart. *The History of Redistricting in the 50 States*. Beverly Hills: Sage Publications, 1981.

Huntingdon, Edward V. *Methods of Apportionment in Congress*. Washington, D.C.: U.S. Government Printing Office, 1940.

Jacobson, Gary C. *The Politics of Congressional Elections*. Boston: Little, Brown, 1983.

Jacobson, Gary C. *The Electoral Origins of Divided Government: Competition in U.S. House Elections, 1946–1988*. Boulder, Col.: Westview Press, 1990.

Jewell, Malcolm E. *The Politics of Reapportionment*. New York: Atherton Press, 1962.

Mann, Thomas E. *Unsafe at Any Margin: Interpreting Congressional Elections*. Washington, D.C.: American Enterprise Institute for Public Policy Research, 1978.

McKay, Robert B. and Howard Scarrow, eds. *Representation and Redistricting Issues in the 1980s*. Lexington, Mass.: Lexington Books, 1981.

National Council of State Legislatures. *Redistricting Provisions: 50 State Profiles.* October 1989.

National Council of State Legislatures. *Reapportionment Law: The 1990s.* Washington, D.C., October 1989.

O'Rourke, Timothy G. *The Impact of Reapportionment.* New Brunswick, N.J.: Transaction Books, 1980.

O'Rourke, Terry B. *Reapportionment; Law, Politics, Computer.* Washington, D.C.: American Enterprise Institute for Public Policy Research, 1972.

Ornstein, Norman; Mann, Thomas E.; and Malbin, Michael J., eds. *Vital Statistics of Congress 1989–1990.* Washington, D.C.: Congressional Quarterly Inc., 1990.

Polsby, Nelson, ed. *Reapportionment in the 1970s.* Berkeley: University of California Press, 1971.

Ponceyri, Robert. *Le Decoupage Electoral.* Collection La Vie Politique. Paris: Economica, 1988.

Stokes, Donald E. *Legislative Reapportionment in New Jersey.* New Brunswick, New Jersey: Report Prepared for the Fund for New Jersey, 1991.

Thernstrom, Abigail M. *Whose Votes Count?: Affirmative Action Minority Voting Rights.* Cambridge, Mass.: Harvard University Press, 1987.

Wollock, Andrea J., ed. *Reapportionment—Law and Technology.* Denver: National Conference of State Legislators, 1980.

Articles

Abromovitz, Alan I. "Partisan Redistricting and the 1982 Congressional Elections." *Journal of Politics* 45 (1983): 776–770.

Baker, Gordon E. "Judicial Determination of Political Gerrymandering: A 'Totality of Circumstances' Approach." *Journal of Law and Politics* 3 (Winter 1989): 1–19.

Basehart, Harry. "The Seats/Votes Relationship and the Identification of Partisan Gerrymandering in State Legislatures." *American Politics Quarterly* 14, no. 4 (1987): 484–494.

Beneson, Robert. "House of the Future at Stake in 1990 Legislative Contests." *Congressional Quarterly* (November 4, 1989): 2971–3003.

Birge, John R. "Redistricting to Maximize the Preservation of Political Boundaries." *Social Science Research* 12 (1983): 205–214.

Born, Richard. "Partisan Intentions and Election Day Realities in the Congressional Redistricting Process." *American Political Science Review* 79 (1985): 305–319.

Brace, Kimball; Grofman, Bernard; and Handley, Lisa. "Does Redistricting Aimed to Help Blacks Necessarily Help Republicans?" *Journal of Politics* 49, no. 1 (February 1987): 169–185.

Brady, David W. and Bernard Grofman. (a) "Swing Ratio, Bias, and the Decline in Electoral Competition in U.S. House Elections 1850–1980, by Regions." Unpublished manuscript, 1988. School of Sciences, University of California, Irvine.

Brady, David and Bernard Grofman. (b) "The Decline in Electoral Competition and the Swing Ratio in U.S. House Elections: 1950–1980." Unpublished paper, 1987. Stanford University.

Bragdon, Peter. "Democrats' Ties to Minorities May Be Test by New Lines." *Congressional Quarterly* (June 2, 1990): 1739–1742.

Browning, Robert X. and Gary King. "Seats, Votes and Gerrymandering: Estimating Representation and Bias in State Legislative Redistricting." *Law and Policy* 9:3 (1987): 305–322.

Buchanan, Robert. "Classic Gerrymander by Indiana Republicans." *Congressional Quarterly* (October 17, 1981): 2017–2022.

Buchanan, Robert. (a) "California GOP Forced to Accept Burton Map." *Congressional Quarterly* (April 24, 1982): 923–942.

Buchanan, Robert. (b) "Minnesota Remap a Democratic Windfall." *Congressional Quarterly* (August 14, 1982): 2000–2005.

Bullock, C.S. and MacManus, Susan A. "Measuring Racial Bloc Voting Is Difficult for Small Jurisdictions." *National Civic Review* 73, no. 7 (July 1984): 336–342.

Bullock, C.S. "The Inexact Science of Congressional Redistricting." *Policy Studies Journal* 15, no. 3 (Summer 1982): 431–496.

Butler, David and Bruce E. Cain. "Reapportionment: A Study in Comparative Government." *Electoral Studies* 4, no. 3 (1985): 197–213.

Cain, Bruce E., and Janet C. Campagna. "Predicting Partisan Congressional Redistricting Plans: The 'Jupiter' Effect." *Legislative Studies Quarterly* 12, no. 2 (May 1987): 265–274.

Cain, Bruce E. "Assessing the Partisan Effects of Redistricting." *American Political Science Review* 79, no. 2 (1985): 320–333.

Campagna, Janet and Bernard Grofman. "Party Control and Partisan Bias in 1980s Congressional Redistricting." Unpublished Paper, 1988. University of California, Irvine.

Colford, Chris. (a) "GOP Apt to Gain Seat in Washington Remap." *Congressional Quarterly* (June 19, 1982): 1472–1478.

Colford, Chris. (b) "Democrats Finagle Best Deal in Kansas Map." *Congressional Quarterly* (July 17, 1982): 1724–1727.

Colford, Chris. (c) "New Connecticut Map Satisfies Both Parties." *Congressional Quarterly* (January 23, 1982): 129–132.

Cook, Rhodes. "New Colorado Map Retains Partisan Balance." *Congressional Quarterly* (July 17, 1982): 1718–1723.

Cook, Rhodes. "Map-Drawers Must Toe the Line in Upcoming Redistricting." *Congressional Quarterly* (September 1, 1990): 2786–2794.

Courtney, J.C. "Theories Masquerading as Principles: Canadian Electoral Boundary Commissions and the Calgary," The Canadian House of Commons: Essays in Honour of Norman Ward. University of Calgary Press, 1985.

Cover, Albert D. and David R. Mayhew. "Congressional Dynamics and the Decline of Competitive Congressional Elections." In *Congress Reconsidered* 2nd ed., edited by Lawrence C. Dodd and Bruce I. Oppenheimer. Washington, D.C.: Congressional Quarterly Press, 1981.

Cover, Albert D. and Bruce S. Brumberg. "Baby Books and Ballots: The Impact of Congressional Mail on Constituent Opinion." *American Political Science Review* 76 (June 1982): 347–359.

Cranor, John D., Gary L. Crawley and Raymond H. Sheele. "The Anatomy of a Gerrymander." *American Journal of Political Science* 33 (1989): 222–239.

Curtice, J. and M. Steed. "Proportionality and Exaggeration in the British Electoral System." *Electoral Studies* 5 (1985): 209–28.

Dixon, Robert G., Jr. "Fair Criteria and Procedures for Establishing Legislative Districts." *Policy Studies Journal* 9, no. 6 (April 1981): 839–850. (Reprinted in *Representation and Redistricting Issues*, edited by B. Grofman, A. Lijphart, R. McKay and H. Scarrow. Lexington, Mass.: Lexington Books, 1982.)

Duncan, Phil. (a) "New Iowa Map: No Gerrymandering Allowed." *Congressional Quarterly* (September 19, 1982): 1798–1801.

Duncan, Phil. (b) "Courts at Odds Over Texas Redistricting." *Congressional Quarterly* (April 3, 1982): 752–762.

Engstrom, Richard L., and Michael D. McDonald. "Quantitative Evidence in Vote Dilution Litigation, Part II: Minority Coalitions and Multivariate Analysis." *The Urban Lawyer* 19, no. 1 (Winter 1987): 175–191.

Erikson, R.S. "Malapportionment, Gerrymandering and Party Fortunes." *American Political Science Review* 66 (1972): 1234–45.

Ferejohn, John A. "On the Decline of Competitive Congressional Elections." *American Political Science Review* 7 (March 1977): 166–76.

Gelman, Andrew and Gary King. "Estimating the Electoral Consequences of Legislative Redistricting." *Journal of the American Statistical Association* 85 (1990): 274.

Gopoian, J. David and Darrel M. West. "Trading Security for Seats: Strategic Considerations in the Redistricting Process." *Journal of Politics* 46 (1984): 1080–1096.

Grofman, Bernard, and Howard A. Scarrow. "Current Issues in Reapportionment." *Law and Policy Quarterly* 4, no. 4 (October 1982): 435–474.

Grofman, Bernard. (a) "Political Gerrymandering: Badham v. Eu, Political Science Goes to Court." *Political Studies* 18 (Summer 1985): 537–581.

Grofman, Bernard. (b) "Criteria for Districting: A Social Science Perspective." *UCLA Law Review* 33 (1985): 77.

King, Gary. "Representation Through Legislative Redistricting: A Stochastic Model." _American Journal of Political Science_ 33 (1988): 787–824.

Light, Larry. (a) "Pennsylvania Map Protects Slight GOP Edge." _Congressional Quarterly_ (May 1, 1982): 995–1005.

Light, Larry. (b) "New Jersey Map Imaginative Gerrymander." _Congressional Quarterly_ (May 22, 1982): 1190–1199.

Light, Larry. (c) "New York Remap Dishes Out Damage Evenly." _Congressional Quarterly_ (August 7, 1982): 1913–1928.

Light, Larry. (d) "New Arizona Districts: A Quandary for Udall." _Congressional Quarterly_ (January 30, 1982): 161–163.

Light, Larry. (e) "New Republican District Created in Utah." _Congressional Quarterly_ (January 2, 1982): 9–11.

Lowenstein, Daniel H. and Jonathan Steinberg. "The Quest for Legislative Districting in the Public Interest: Elusive or Illusory?" _UCLA Law Review_ 33 (1985): 1–75.

Mayhew, David R. "Congressional Elections: The Case of the Vanishing Marginals." _Policy_ (1974): 298–302.

McCubbins, M.D., and Thomas Schwartz. "Congress, the Courts, and Public Policy: Consequences of the One Man, One Vote Rule." _American Journal of Political Science_ 32, no. 2 (May 1988): 388–415.

Menendez, Albert. "Racial Issue Dominates Georgia Redistricting." _Congressional Quarterly_ (December 5, 1981): 2403–2407.

Niemi, Richard G. and John Deegan, Jr. "A Theory of Political Districting." _American Political Science Review_ 72 (1978): 1304–1323.

Niemi, Richard G. "The Effects of Districting Trade-Offs Among Party Competition, Electoral Responsiveness and Seats-Votes Relationships." In _Representation and Redistricting Issues_, edited by B. Grofman, A. Lijphart, R. McKay, and H. Scarrow. Lexington, Mass.: Lexington Books, 1982.

Niemi, Richard G. "The Relationship Between Seats and Votes: The Ultimate Question in Political Gerrymandering." _UCLA Law Review_ 33, no. 1 (1985): 401–423.

Niemi, Richard G. and Stephen Wright. "Majority Win Percentages: An Approach to the Votes-Seats Relationship in Light of *Davis v. Bandemer*." In *Toward Fair and Effective Representation: Political Gerrymandering and the Courts*. Bernard Grofman, ed. New York: Agathon Press, 1989.

Owen, Guillermo and Bernard Grofman. "Optimal Partisan Gerrymandering." *Political Geography Quarterly* 7, no. 1 (1988): 5–22.

Pachon, Harry. "U.S. Citizenship and Latino Participation in California Politics," pp. 71–88. *Racial and Ethnic Politics in California*, Byran A. Jackson and Michael B. Preston, eds. Berkeley: IGS Press, 1991.

Pytte, Alyson. "U.S. Census: More's at Stake Than Just Counting Heads." *Congressional Quarterly* (May 5, 1990): 1337–1341.

Robertson, A. "American Redistricting in the 1980s: The Effect on the Mid-Term Elections." *Electoral Studies* 2, no. 2 (August 1983): 113–29.

Scarrow, Howard. "The Impact of Reapportionment on Party Representation in the State of New York." *Policy Studies Journal* Special Issue on Reapportionment 9, no. 6 (April 1981): 937–946.

Scarrow, Howard. "One Voter, One Vote: The Apportionment of Congressional Seats Reconsidered." *Policy* (Winter 1989): 253–268.

Schuck, Peter. "What Went Wrong with the Voting Rights Act?" *Washington Monthly* (November 1983): 51–56.

Still, Edward. "Alternatives to Single-Member Districts." In *Minority Vote Dilution*, edited by C. Davidson. Washington, D.C.: Howard University Press, 1984.

"Symposium: Gerrymandering and the Courts." *UCLA Law Review* 33 (October 1985): 1–281.

Tufte, E. "Determinants of the Outcome of Mid-Term Congressional Elections." *APSR* 69 (1972): 816–826.

Waller, R.J. "The 1983 Boundary Commission: Policies and Effects." *Electoral Studies* 2, no. 3 (December 1983): 195–206.

Young, H.P. "Measuring the Compactness of Legislative Districts." *Legislative Studies Quarterly* 13, no. 1 (February 1988): 105–116.

INDEX